DESIGNER'S PREPRESS COMPANION

Jessica Berlin
Christina Kim
Jennifer Talcott

with Frank J. Romano

NAPL

National Association for Printing Leadership
Paramus, New Jersey

Printed in the USA.

Senior Staff Director, Communications: Dawn A. Lospaluto
Director, Publications: Richard S. Papale

Editors: Erika Kendra, Elisabeth C. Sydor; *Editorial Assitant:* Andra Bell

Cover Design: Jennifer Arbaiza

Some of the illustrations are copyright Frank J. Romano
and used with his permission

ISBN 1-929734-25-5

CONTENTS

CHAPTER 1

INTRODUCTION

From the very first sketch, today's designer must keep in mind the technical requirements the design will encounter along the way. Modern graphic artists use sophisticated software that permits designs to be executed in days, that before would have taken weeks. But with this creative freedom comes the need to understand and be accountable for how the design will work within the technical requirements of the printing process.

Prepress design is now truly a comprehensive stage of the printing process that demands technical know-how, microscopic attention to detail, and the constant awareness of tempering the design to a printer's capabilities. The more a designer can learn how to accommodate the printing process, whether traditional or digital, the more the designer will ensure producing a design that is not only compelling, pleasing, and commercially viable, but is printable — and profitable for all concerned.

Begin with the end in mind — and understand the steps in between — and your design will be successful. This book is written to help you along the way.

BRAINSTORMING YOUR DESIGN

The first stage of a design job is to learn about the client, their goals, and their preferences. Some clients allow you to influence their look, but more often you are required to design within your client's comfort zone. During this research phase, write down key words that give you a feel for the company and their products.

THINKING AND THUMBNAILS

Take three words that reflect the company and try to generate designs that reflect those words. Next, grab pencil and paper and sketch; generate as many idea sketches as possible. Start with logic in the research phase, and then let the creative side of your mind take over and shape the logic into innovative ideas.

Figure 1-1. Thumbnail Sketches.
These can and should be quick and rough. Just generate ideas, worry about refining them later.

Thumbnails should only be two inches or so tall — quick little drawings made with a marker; stark black against the white of the page will give a better indication of how the design might look than with a pencil.

ROUGHS

After you have two or three pages of thumbnail sketches, walk away. Take the three best ideas from your thumbnails and make more detailed drawings. At this stage, generate larger sketches. Keep them rough; you want an idea of where you should invest your time. If you need to think about what fonts to use, print your main words in various fonts. Get feedback from other designers if you can, or

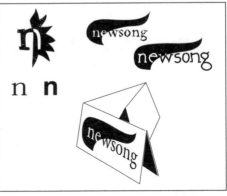

Figure 1-2. Roughs.
Take a couple of your thumbnails and refine them.

from people who are not designers. Ask what they like, what draws their eye, what bothers them, which they would rather view all day, and so on.

If you are making a book or a brochure, create a mock-up. Start folding paper to the exact sizes you may want to use. Create a sample and sketch ideas on the pages.

COMPREHENSIVE MOCK-UPS (COMPS)

Finally, you can jump onto your computer and generate refined ideas. You may want to just work on the strongest of your three rough ideas, or try out all three. Try all the subtle shifts in placement or color that make a design truly snap. Everything looks different on paper, so remember to print your ideas, starting in black and white. Color quickly seduces and will interfere with the objective assessment of placement and design needed at this stage.

Color versions are appropriate for presenting comps at your second client meeting; the client may want to see the roughs too. The thumbnails will not be necessary. You can include photos from the Web or stock photos, but remember to build these into your cost estimate.

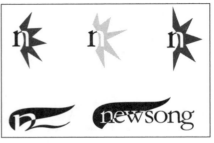

Figure 1-3. Comps. At this stage, the computer is ideal for trying different ideas.

Figure 1-4. Mock-ups. You want to create versions that will reflect the finished product.

ORGANIZATION

As you begin to generate ideas, including images, text, and so on, set up a job folder on your computer desktop. Inside that folder, create one folder for images, one for fonts; leave the layout within the job folder, but outside the internal folders. This is one way to insure that your layout file always links properly to images that are stored in the image folder.

Some designers keep just the current jobs on the desktop. Once pieces are published, they burn the job to a CD for archiving. Make sure that you burn both layered and final versions of the job in case you need to go back and make any changes.

EDITORIAL INPUT

Your client may love your ideas, take them home, show them around, and then change their mind and ask for significant rework. Here is the human element in all its frustration and glory. Be patient.

One good policy to develop up front with a client, before any design is done, is that they get three stages of input within your original cost estimate:

1. The first stage is for major changes: a different image or symbol, a change in size or typeface, new colors, etc.

2. The second stage includes lesser changes (after you implement their major changes): a shift in headline placement, minor changes in wording, a switch in quotes, etc.

3. The third stage only allows for typo changes.

If the client wants more changes than that, let them know that they will be charged appropriately. People will often continue to make changes, so make sure to build in the cost at the front end.

If the client wants the color of the entire brochure shifted from blue to mauve just before you hand it to the printer, it's okay; but they should be

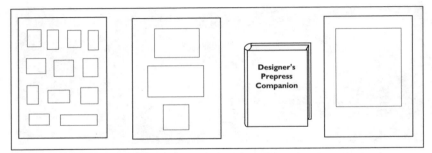

Figure 1-5. Brainstorming Your Design. First generate thumbnails, then roughs. Next check your idea with an expert, usually the print provider; then create comprehensive drafts of your design.

charged because these changes are outside your initial contract. Put all this in writing and have them sign it before you start designing. Have this and any other contractual concerns pre-printed on the back of your estimate page, and make sure the client reads and signs off on your contractual concerns before you proceed.

PREPRESS WORKFLOWS

In the final development stages, don't hesitate to discuss some of your ideas with the printer. Doing so will help ensure the job is printed effectively and efficiently.

Different firms will have different workflows. You may not always have time to follow each of the stages outlined here. If you can only jot down ten quick sketches before jumping onto the computer, at least do that. You will be pleasantly surprised at the creative ideas you will generate.

CHAPTER 2

OFFSET LITHOGRAPHY: PRINTING WITH CHEMISTRY

Lithography, in particular *offset lithography*, is one of the main printing processes used in graphic design. This process is used for most professional brochures, stationery (envelopes, letterhead, business cards), booklets, books, promotional pieces, newspapers, and annual reports. Lithography is high-quality, usually four-color (or more) printing.

WHAT IS LITHOGRAPHY?

As a child, did you ever draw with crayon on paper and then paint over it with watercolor? Remember how the water would not cover what you had already colored with the oily wax of the crayon? That is the basic concept used in lithography. You put down an oily area that will repel water; after a coating of water, the ink gets attracted to the area without water and when you print, the water evaporates and the ink remains on the paper.

image courtesy Graphic Arts Technical Foundation

Figure 2-1. Lithography Stones with Chemically Produced Images.

FINE-ART LITHOGRAPHY

Before the big machines of offset, lithography used oil crayons on stone. Fine-art lithography starts with a limestone (*lithos* in Greek), which is drawn on with an oil stick. The stone is then etched (cut into) with acid. Thereafter, the entire image is washed away along with the acid. The oil-stick sections are now oil receptive, and the other parts of the stone will absorb water. After the stone is wetted, ink is rolled over the stone; the ink sticks to the previously drawn areas, and is then transferred to paper in a press.

A number of impressions can be printed from the same drawing because of how the surface of the stone has been affected. Alois Senefelder, a Bavarian playwright, figured out this method in 1798.

HOW LITHOGRAPHY WORKS NOW

Printing plates are now made of aluminum sheets instead of limestone. Printable areas are created with a bunch of tiny dots on the metal plate; even straight lines are made of tiny dots set close together. Because the process is chemical, you cannot actually feel a difference in the areas with dots (the *image area*) and the areas without dots (the *non-image area*).

OFFSETTING THE IMAGE

The major difference between fine-art lithography and modern lithographic printing (other than metal plates) is the use of a *blanket cylinder*. Instead of the plate printing directly onto the paper, an extra rubber cylinder receives the image and then transfers it to the paper (or whatever substrate). Thus the name *offset* — the printed image is transferred, or offset, onto the blanket before going onto the paper.

Why bother, you ask? The blanket roller means that the plate does not directly contact the paper. Paper is surprisingly abrasive. Think of it as a lot

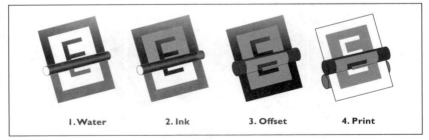

| 1. Water | 2. Ink | 3. Offset | 4. Print |

Figure 2-2. The Offset Lithography Process.

1. Wet an aluminum plate with water
2. Ink the plate
3. Transfer ink from the plate to the blanket cylinder
4. Transfer ink from the blanket cylinder onto the substrate (i.e., paper)

of ground-up wood chips, with the ability to scratch a plate. Using a blanket cylinder allows printing plates to last longer and to gain flexibility. The blanket cylinder is made of rubber and applies ink evenly to various

Figure 2-3. Right and Wrong Reading.

substrates: coated or uncoated paper, plastic, metal, cardboard, and so on.

Another advantage to offsetting the image is a right-reading printing plate. A lithographic plate reads like what will appear on paper, which allows mistakes to (hopefully) be caught before going to press. Although a better place to do your proofreading is at the earlier, less expensive proofing stage.

It is possible to read any text when the plate is made, thus the name right-reading. The image is transferred, wrong-reading, to the blanket cylinder, and from there it is printed right-reading onto the substrate.

SCREENS AND MOIRÉ

There are two basic ways to distribute dots on the printing plate, AM (amplitude modulated) and FM (frequency-modulated) screening. Before discussing the differences between AM and FM, let's discuss *line screens*. Line screens are used to render *continuous-tone* images into printable *halftone* dots. These screens have a certain number of *lines per inch*, or lpi. In order to make a printing plate, a line screen is placed over the film. The finer the line screen, the more lines per inch it will have. As you can see in Figure 2-4, 150 lpi produces some very small dots.

There are two different kinds of screens currently in use. *Amplitude modulated* (AM) screening is when line-screen dots are distributed evenly. Only the size or shape of the dot varies; highlights are tiny dots and shadows are big dots. *Frequency modulated* (FM) screening (often and incorrectly called stochastic screening), means that the dots are all the same size: highlights have few dots and shadows have lots of dots. An FM screen looks like an airbrush piece, while an AM screen looks like pointillism.

FM screening allows more than four colors to be printed without moiré being a problem. *Moiré* (pronounced mÔ-ray) is an interference pattern that happens when the dots form a visible pattern within an image.

Each AM screen has to be set at different angles to avoid creating such a pattern. Unfortunately, adding a new color to an AM-screened job makes it nearly impossible to avoid moiré.

Moiré happens when a picture has objects in a repeating pattern, such as a fence. Since the dot placement is randomized in FM screening, no patterns are created; thus there is no moiré to fuss with. This has contributed to the

Figure 2-4. 10 and 20 lpi are not usually used in the printing industry; they are shown here so that you can see the dot pattern in the screen. 85–110 lpi screens are used for newspaper images; 110–175 are common for higher-end lithography. LPI is preset, so this is not a value that you can pick and choose. The printer will select this option based on the capabilities of the press they are using.

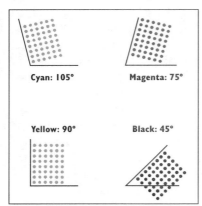

Cyan: 105°   **Magenta: 75°**

Yellow: 90°   **Black: 45°**

Figure 2-5. Line Screen Angles. To avoid creating a moiré pattern, AM line screens are set to different angles depending on the plate color. Since a 90° pattern is the strongest visually, the lightest color, yellow, is placed at 90° and the others arranged accordingly. If you look at a printed sheet with a magnifying glass or loupe, you may be able to pick out the angles.

explosion of five-, six-, and eight-color presses. The disadvantage of FM screening is that midtones can look darker than the same area in AM screens. When too many layers of colored dots get piled together, it is harder to keep midtones light and still detailed.

WEBFED VS. SHEETFED

Offset lithography has two press options, *webfed* and *sheetfed*, which relate to how the substrate is fed into the printing press. Webfed presses use rolls of paper that are automatically pulled through the printing units. A web press is usually also *perfecting*, printing both sides of the paper at once.

A sheetfed press, on the other hand, has an automatic paper feeder that puts one sheet of paper into the press at a time. The paper moves through the different color units and then out the other

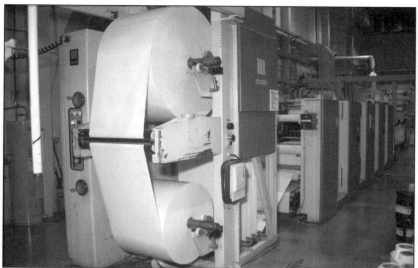

Figure 2-6. Webfed presses are faster than sheetfed, but need a longer job run (i.e., greater number of copies) before they are economical. Webfed presses are usually perfecting (printing both sides of the sheet at once).

Figure 2-7. Sheetfed presses feed into the press from a stack of pre-cut paper. The paper is cut by the paper manufacturer. Because of how the sheet is fed through the press, there needs to be enough space for a gripper edge (usually 0.125 inch, or 3 mm). Sheetfed presses often print one side at a time, though perfecting presses are available.

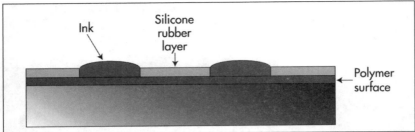

Figure 2-8. A cross-section of a waterless plate. In a conventional plate, water would fill in the non-image gaps before the ink is laid down; a waterless plate has a layer of silicone that will not accept the ink (the silicone is oleophobic, meaning ink-hating).

end. Sheetfed presses often only print one side at a time, making them slower than webfed presses. Because of this, any high-volume printing goes on a web press — catalogs, newspapers, some magazines, and some books. These products are often of lower quality than those printed on a sheetfed press.

WATERLESS LITHOGRAPHY
In the last forty years, great strides have been made in developing a form of lithography that needs no water. *Waterless lithography* uses a silicone plastic in non-image areas. Instead of water filling in the non-image area, the plastic repels the ink. In many ways, this is an exciting advance in the industry. Because no water is involved, the paper gets less saturated, which in turn means that more ink (proportionally) can be used. More ink means more density, better coverage, and more brilliant color.

Getting the ink and water into the proper balance can take a while; the *makeready* is much shorter for waterless, which saves time and expense. This process is also environmentally friendly because less solvents need to be used, and the drying time is shorter. Waterless lithography also has less dot gain, which allows designs to print more crisply with finer lines.

The bad news is that waterless plates are more delicate, which makes the process more expensive than regular lithography (the client may never see a price savings on makeready). You may want to consider using waterless lithography when the details of your job are vital — annual reports, certain brochures, and the like.

"HI-FI" OR HEXACHROME COLORS
Hi-Fi (or *Hexachrome*, which is Pantone's version) color refers to printing with more than four colors of ink. "Hi-Fi" is short for *high-frequency color*, which refers to FM screening where the frequency of dots is changed instead of size. Printers add more breadth and depth to color by using extra units of the press. Some add pure versions of red, green, and blue as extra colors.

Pantone's Hexachrome system uses Vivid Orange and Vibrant Green as the extra colors. Pantone claims that, with those two colors, they are able to duplicate a large portion of their spot colors since the extra colors increase the color gamut. This adds extra expense, but is justifiable for some jobs.

Clothing catalogs, sewing and thread catalogs, and the like are examples of jobs that will benefit from Hi-Fi color — anywhere that the print color must match an actual object. An eight-color press allows you to specify spot colors for your job that will let you come close to what you see on screen. When you are at the rough draft stage, call around and ask various printers if Hi-Fi color is appropriate for your job. One of the primary technical problems in Hi-Fi print is a lack of proofing devices. Most proofing systems only have four colors, though a six-color proofer is available; if a printer specializes in Hi-Fi, ask if the company has a way to proof more than four colors.

ADVANTAGES AND DISADVANTAGES OF LITHOGRAPHY

WHEN SHOULD YOU USE LITHOGRAPHY?

As we mentioned in the introduction, lithography is used for magazines, newspapers, books, booklets, professional brochures, stationery sets (envelopes, letterhead, business cards), promotional pieces, and annual reports. Use lithography for run lengths between 1,000 and 500,000, and when you want large quantities printed at high speed.

SPEED AND SIZE

Sheetfed lithography is relatively slow, but still is much faster than any digital press. A sheetfed press may print 10,000–12,000 sheets an hour, and some sheetfed presses can handle large sheets of paper. Webfed presses are even faster than sheetfed. They print most books, daily newspapers, and many magazines. Web rolls can be as wide as five feet (1.5 meter), and print 3,000 feet per minute. The limitation for lithography is that the image can be wide, but can be no longer than the biggest blanket and printing cylinders. Because the plates are aluminum sheets, the ends are bent and secured into the cylinder; the same is true of the blanket cylinder, which creates a gap in the print.

IMAGE AND COLOR QUALITY

Part of the mystery and magic of printing is how four basic colors broken up into tiny dots can fool the eye into seeing thousands of colors. Hi-fi color is starting to offer broader color gamuts for lithography, but color is still relatively limited for most printing processes. A four-color lithographic press will not reproduce neon colors and the like, nor will the other traditional printing processes. Different inks are used for different printing options so the color gamuts will vary, but you are limited to the gamut of that ink set.

If printed within the proper gamut, lithographic presses are capable of handsome color. Solid areas of color will usually print consistently. Lithography produces very fine image detail, but for broad areas of flat screen colors you may want to pick a custom or spot ink. Any mix of the four-color inks will have some variation, especially at a tinted level; it would be better to specify a custom ink at 100%. If the cost of an extra unit on press would take you over budget, and you still want to use screened tints as a design element, choose a tint made with only one or two process colors.

MAKEREADY AND COST

One of the disadvantages of lithography is how long it takes before a job is printing acceptably. Lithography has a fixed, high cost of setup called *make-ready*. This includes how long it takes to generate films and plates, how long it takes to get the ink and water in balance on the press, and the cost of wasted ink and paper. Due to the chemical nature of the process, it takes a while to get the ink and water into proper balance. Printers have figured out many techniques to spread the cost of makeready over the job. That is why when you ask for a quote for 100,000 brochures, they might send you a quote for 100,000, 125,000, 150,000, and 175,000 copies. Once the press is running properly, it may be an hour or less to print another 25,000 copies — thus the adage, "The more you print, the less it costs."

DOT GAIN

Lithographic printing plates are aluminum sheets with lots of tiny dots. Those inked dots are transferred to the blanket roll and from there to the sub-strate. Predictably, as the dots are transferred they get smashed a bit, which leads to *dot gain*. The term also refers to the gain in size as the image moves from film, through scanning, and into the printing process.

There is a range of dot gain in lithography. Web presses have higher dot gain than sheetfed; dot gain increases still more if an uncoated paper is used because the paper absorbs the ink more than coated paper, causing the ink to spread out. Think of doing ink washes on newsprint versus bond paper; which one makes the ink spread more? The standard dot gain for web offset as defined in SWOP (Specifications for Web Offset Publications) is 20%. Some sheetfed presses with coated papers have lower values for dot gain, while newsprint has dot gain around 30%.

Figure 2-9. Dot Gain.
A 40% dot looks on film (left) like a 57% dot once printed (right). That means that there is a dot gain of 17%. The squares around the dot represent the area of a theoretical 100% size dot.

Figure 2-10. Paper Absorption and Dot Gain. There are different causes of dot gain. One of them is how much ink is absorbed by the paper. The gray band represents the paper; the black represents the ink dots. Some of the ink lies above the surface, some is absorbed. Uncoated paper will absorb more ink (think of a paper towel versus wax paper).

images courtesy Graphic Arts Technical Foundation

Figure 2-11. Allowing for Dot Gain. The image on the left allowed for the dot gain on the press; the image on the right shows what occurs without that allowance. When the correct dot gain settings are used in prepress, the final result looks fine.

Fortunately, compensation for dot gain can happen at the prepress stage, so that the image looks great in the end. If a press has been measured, or *profiled*, and is known to have 17% dot gain, prepress can preset the 40% dot to 27% (for example). Then after a 17% gain, the dot would end up at 40%. Most of the time, all we have to do is set up the right numbers in our files (see Chapter 18).

DRYING

Since lithographic inks are formed from oils and solvents, they need a fair amount of drying time. If insufficient drying time is allowed, some heavily coated areas may not dry and may cause binding and finishing problems. This is a particular problem if individual books are perfect bound while the ink is still not dry, and then shrink wrapped and shipped. When the plastic is split open, the books have been known to fall apart because the ink solvent migrated into the adhesive and broke the glue bond.

INK TYPES

The default ink set used in lithography is SWOP, which applies to magazine printing — *Time, Newsweek*, and so on. The inks used in different lithographic presses vary in thickness, tack, and hue; as an example, newspaper printing uses different inks than the SWOP set.

All inks do share some characteristics — they are oil-based, very sticky, and thick. If you turn an open can of lithographic ink over, the ink will never drip, ooze, or fall out; it has to be pulled out. The ink is formed that way so that it will stay a consistent thickness and stickiness as it runs through all the rollers in the *ink train*. The stickiness of the ink contributes to some of the print defects particular to lithography.

PRINTING DEFECTS

- **Mechanical ghosting** Mechanical ghosting can be avoided by not having a dense four-color image above or next to an area that requires minimal ink coverage in one of the colors. If the plate is loaded up with color for one area, it may not have enough for the lighter area that comes next, or it may have extra ink that it deposits in that light area. You may get less ink in the lighter area, which is called ghosting.

- **Gloss ghosting** Gloss ghosting occurs particularly in sheetfed jobs. While drying in a stack, the evaporating solvent will occasionally leave a ghost image on the bottom of the next sheet up in the stack.

- **Blanket smash** With blanket smash, if the offset blanket gets banged up, it may get a dent that will not print. Those white areas are blanket smash.

- **Mottle** Mottle is a random, uneven pattern on the paper. The printer will try different remedies, but in the end you may need to pick a different paper.

- **Show-through** Show-through occurs when the paper is thin enough that the color on one side of the sheet affects the appearance of the other side of the sheet. Pick a different, thicker paper.

- **Ink droplets** If a drop of ink lands where it should not, it will show as a streak as it is dragged between the blanket and the plate.

- **Hickies** Hickies are little halo marks that are a result of dirt or paper particles that have stuck to the blanket. The press operator has to wash the blanket to eliminate hickies.

- **Picking** Picking is a problem interrelated with hickies. Picking happens when the ink is sticky enough to pull up little bits of paper. Just like trying to remove a sticker from a sheet of paper, it leads to little rips in the printed sheet. If those picked pieces of paper stay on the blanket, they will cause hickies.

- **Blistering** Blistering occurs on coated paper in heavily printed areas. The ink underneath is unable to dry, or gets under the coating of the paper, causing a raised blister on the printed sheet.

- **Scuffing** Scuffing is a result of abrasions that penetrate through varnish and coated stock to show the paper.

- **Misting (or flying)** Misting occurs from drops of ink being thrown from the roller. They look like tiny smashed dots of ink that are in places they should not be.

- **Dry-up** Dry-up is when ink bleeds into non-image areas because there was not enough water on the plate.

DESIGN CONSIDERATIONS

Registration means having all plates hit the paper at the right time so that the colors line up correctly and without any shifting around. It is difficult to keep pages in registration on any press, although printers do it all the time. It is amazing that they can control such huge, high-speed machines to such a fine degree. Out-of-registration images often occur in catalogs, and in color newspaper photos. The colors in the pictures seem to shift, while type is still legible. It just means the paper did not hit the blanket cylinder at the exact moment it needed to. Some design issues particular to lithography include:

- Because of registration issues, use a single, 100% tint, solid color for text size type and for thin lines. Photographic images can absorb very slight registration variations, but a four-color hairline is unforgiving.

- Some common page sizes used in sheetfed lithography:
  Text paper: 23 × 35 in.   Cover paper: 25 × 38 in.
  Do not forget to ask which direction the grain goes, long or short; it can be ordered in either direction.

- Do not fill the entire sheet with a design; there needs to be room for the *gripper edge*, a small mechanical grip that moves the sheet through the press. As a general rule, leave 0.25 in. The printer also needs to put color quality-control bars on the sheet. Ask ahead how much space you can consume with your design.

- In both sheetfed and webfed jobs, you may not save any money by using one color on one side and four colors on the other side of a sheet. The job would have to use just two colors throughout to save any money, since this kind of job is usually printed on a less expensive two-color press instead of a four-color (or more) press. Ask in advance how much the savings would be, and decide from the beginning if it is worth it to give up color options for the cost savings that may be available.

- Use a *rich black* in any solid black fill areas. A rich black consists of more than just 100% black. Usually it is a blend of over 90% black and percentages of the other colors. This creates more even coverage and a deeper color tone. Just make sure any reversed type is big enough (10-pt. sans serif and 12-pt. serif are usually fine).

- If you are using FM screening, make sure the paper you select has a very smooth finish. FM dots are so small that they disappear into the crevices of a textured sheet. High-quality coated stock is your best bet, though smooth-finished uncoated paper can also work.

- Yellow can disappear if you don't add a hint of magenta, which of course gives it a hint of orange. Straight yellow is possible with a fifth color unit that uses fluorescent yellow ink. Or, you could ask your printer to mix some fluorescent ink into the process ink fountain.

CHAPTER 3

LETTERPRESS & FLEXOGRAPHY: PRINTING UNDER PRESSURE

Letterpress and flexography are both *relief printing*, which means that the image areas for printing are raised; pressure is used to imprint the image or text onto a substrate.

HOW RELIEF PRINTING WORKS

Think back to first grade art class, and the time you cut a potato into the shape of a star, covered it with paint, and used it as a stamp. Relief printing works the same way, using printing plates that have raised and non-raised areas. A printing plate is the surface, whether metal or a type of polymer, that is etched or chemically engraved to produce the image to be reproduced by a printing process. The raised parts of the printing plates both receive ink and come into contact with the surface being printed. The images are also reversed on the printing plate, or *wrong reading*, as shown in Figure 3-1.

HOW DID IT COME ABOUT?

Letterpress (of sorts) was the first form of printing, even predating Gutenberg's moveable type. Printing was invented centuries earlier in the orient. The Chinese and Koreans carved pages of text out of wood and printed on rice paper. Gutenberg cast type in metal and set it into lines of text on flat surfaces. Ink was applied to the surface with rollers and a piece of paper was pressed down onto it. Because of the pressure involved in the process, you can actually feel a slight indent on words printed using letterpress printing.

Figure 3-1. Basic Principle of Relief Printing.

LETTERPRESS

How Does It Work?

The parts of the plate to be printed are raised. Inked rollers are rolled over the plate. Ink is transferred to the raised areas of the plate. The printing plate comes into contact with the printing surface, and the ink is transferred onto the paper.

What Do You Use It For?

Letterpress is no longer used as much as it once was — it was once the most popular form of printing. However, it is still what most people envision when they think of printing. It is not really used at all in commercial printing, but it is still used in some very small print houses for newspapers, or for aesthetic reasons when typesetting books by hand.

What Are the Limitations and Advantages?

Letterpress printing has considerable makeready time, but compared to lithography, far less. The makeready time for letterpress mostly involves typesetting the metal or wood type. Letterpress images are crisp and sharp, but due to the pressure of the impact, there tends to be a heavier edge around letterforms.

FLEXOGRAPHY

How Does It Work?

The main difference between the two relief processes is that flexography uses a flexible plate typically made from a *photopolymer*, which is nothing more than light-sensitive plastic.

Ink is applied to an anilox roller. The *anilox roller* is made up of tiny cells that fill with ink. A *doctor blade* removes excess ink from the anilox roller in a two-roller system, or a fountain roller reduces excess ink in a three-roller system. The ink in the cells from the anilox roller is transferred to raised image areas on the plate cylinder. The non-image areas are not raised and therefore will not receive any ink. The plate and impression cylinders sandwich the substrate and transfer ink onto the paper. Just like with lithography's SWOP

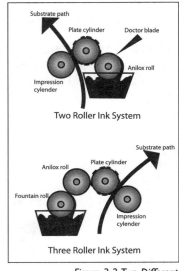

Figure 3-2. Two Different Flexographic Ink Systems.

standards, flexography has its own set of standards called FIRST (Flexographic Image Reproduction Specifications and Tolerances).

WHAT DO YOU USE IT FOR?

Flexography is very popular for package printing. The process can print on a wide variety of substrates that many other machines cannot:

- Paper/paperboard — These include corrugated boards, solid bleached sulfate and recycled paperboard (folding cartons), coated papers (labels and gift wrapping), and uncoated sheetfed (paperback books).

- Polymer films — Polyethylene (dry cleaner bags, candy wrappers), polypropylene (snack food packages, candy wrappers), and polyvinyl chloride (wall coverings).

- Multilayer/laminations — Metallized papers (gift wrapping) and films (snack food bags), and polyethylene coated SBS (milk cartons).

WHAT ARE THE LIMITATIONS AND ADVANTAGES?

Flexography does not always appear sharp for images with fine detail because it lacks fine screen ruling. Due to the contact between the printing plate and the paper or substrate, the halftone dots that make up the image grow larger around the edges and plugging occurs in the shadow areas. That means there is less detail in the shadows; a dark object, such as a black cat, can look like a dark shape instead of a cat.

Dot gain and misregistration are greater in flexography than in offset lithography. Subtle highlight details may not print because the highlight dots on the plate may not transfer ink much of the time, leaving the paper white where ink should be; any detail will range from little to none. Try to avoid designs that use large amounts of highlights. Flexography also has a tendency for color variation due to the nature of the printing process and of flexographic inks.

Flexography is capable of laying down very dense layers of ink to achieve the look of screen printing. The ink is fast-drying and allows the machine to run at high speeds. The plates are cheap and makeready time is short. The advances in photopolymer technology have improved the image quality in flexography, but it is still not comparable to lithographic image quality.

The ink used in flexography is either a fast-drying water-based ink or a non-solvent ink. Both types of flexographic inks are more environmentally friendly then the oil-based inks used in other printing processes. They are also safer for use on wrappers that come in direct contact with foods.

DESIGN CONSIDERATIONS

COLOR

Since much of flexography is printed on brown Kraft linerboard, color matching is harder to achieve due to the initial color of the substrates. This is important to remember when viewing prints, especially if the proofs are not on the actual substrate the job will be printed on.

Keep in mind that if you are creating packaging for cauliflower on a plastic bag, the white cauliflower may look a bit gray because flexography prints a highlight dot at 10%, where lithography can print it at 3%.

Due to the problem with highlight dots in flexography, vignettes are almost impossible. Printing an image that fades away to a white paper will cause a hash line where the highlight edge falls.

TYPOGRAPHY

Fine lines like those in type tend to grow in size during printing because of the soft and flexible nature of flexographic plates. Negative or reverse type tends to pinch or fill in; however, this only occurs in situations with poor equipment and difficult substrates.

Depending on the substrate used, there are limitations on point size. Small type with serifs are the most difficult. Whenever possible, use a sans-serif typeface in flexographic printing. It is important to discuss with your printer any limitations of the substrate you are printing on. It is possible, depending on the problem, to compensate by choosing a lighter or heavier typeface.

As a rule of thumb for wide-web printing, use 6-pt. type minimum, and 9-pt. type minimum for reversed type. For narrow-web printing, use 4-pt. type minimum, and 6-pt. type minimum for reversed type.

CHAPTER 4

GRAVURE: PRINTING WITH HOLES

Gravure, or *rotogravure*, is industrial *intaglio* printing, which involves transferring an image from a sunken surface. The image to be printed is etched or engraved below the surface of the image carrier, or *gravure cylinder*. To put it in simpler terms, gravure is printing using a cylinder with holes in it. This may sound strange and difficult, but it is really a simple printing process.

HOW GRAVURE WORKS

The gravure printing process uses an ink fountain, gravure/image cylinder, impression cylinder, and a doctor blade. The gravure cylinder is etched or engraved with a pattern of tiny cells or holes. The cells are etched or engraved at varying depths and widths to produce the different tones in an image; they hold the ink and put the image onto the paper or other substrate. The deep cells hold more ink and produce the darker, or shadow, areas of the image. The shallow cells hold smaller amounts of ink and produce the lighter, or highlight, areas of an image.

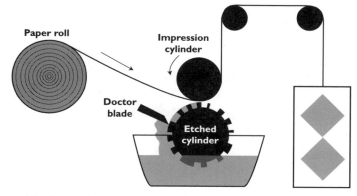

Figure 4-1. The Gravure Process.

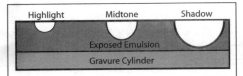

Figure 4-2. Varying Cell Depths.

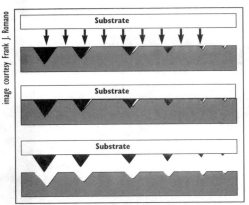

Figure 4-3. Ink is pulled from cells to the substrate when cylinders are pressed together.

The gravure cylinder is partially submerged in an ink fountain and is rotated to pick up ink in the engraved cells. A doctor blade then scrapes against the surface of the gravure cylinder to remove any ink on the non-image area, or parts of the cylinder that do not have engraved cells and do not transfer ink to the substrate.

The substrate is passed between the gravure cylinder and the impression cylinder; ink that remains in the cells is transferred to the substrate from the pressure created by the two cylinders. In other words, the gravure and impression cylinders squeeze together and force the ink out of the cells onto the paper. The printed paper then moves through a drying unit to fix the ink to the paper.

WHAT IS GRAVURE USED FOR?

Gravure is used for nearly twenty percent of all printing done in the United States. It is typically used for three types of printing:

- **Packaging printing** Bags, boxes, labels, folding cartons, gift wrappers.

- **Publication printing** Catalogs, magazines, newspaper supplements, mass mailing advertisements. Magazines with a large subscription base, anything over one or two million copies, often choose to print on a gravure press; *National Geographic* is one example.

- **Product printing** Printing of materials such as vinyl, wallpaper, floor coverings, textiles.

ADVANTAGES AND DISADVANTAGES OF GRAVURE

SPEED AND SIZE

One of the many advantages of gravure printing is the size and speed of gravure presses. They are the largest and fastest running presses today, ranging in width from under 12 in. to as wide as 265 in. (6.7 meters or roughly 22 feet). This allows for printing on various substrates, including sheet vinyl for floor covering.

Gravure press speeds are extremely fast and are limited mainly by the substrate used. Publication presses typically operate at a speed of 3,000 feet per minute. Depending on the product being printed, packaging presses usually run at half the speed of publication presses. Gravure has the highest continuous operating speeds of any commercial press.

GRAVURE CYLINDER

Another advantage to gravure is the image carrier, or the gravure cylinder. The majority of gravure cylinders are made with steel as the base material, which is then coated with copper to give the cylinder engravability, stability, and reproducibility. Copper can easily be engraved and the image remains stable even under the high *nip pressure*, or the pressure created between the gravure cylinder and the impression cylinder. Copper can also be removed from the cylinder and replaced so that the cylinder can be used again.

In addition to the copper coating, the cylinder is coated with chrome to allow for longer press runs. Chrome gives the copper surface of the cylinder more durability by protecting it from the abrasive wear caused by the friction created at the *nip*, or the place where the gravure cylinder and the impression cylinder meet and pull the substrate through.

The gravure cylinder also has an advantage over the image carriers of other printing processes because it is a *gapless cylinder*, which means that the image can go completely around the cylinder. Lithography plates take up only a portion of the cylinder so that there is space to fasten the plate to the cylinder, and there is a gap where nothing is being printed as the cylinder rotates.

The gapless gravure cylinder allows continuous prints and results in a minimal amount of unprinted space. This reduces substrate waste and saves money. The ability of the gapless cylinder to achieve a continuous print or pattern makes gravure ideal for printing items such as wallpaper and textiles. The gapless cylinder also allows for many different image layout options, including random and nested images.

GRAVURE INKS

Gravure inks provide another advantage to this printing process. Because the gravure cylinder is resistant to virtually all chemicals, inks can be formulated to print on any substrate. Gravure inks are also fast drying, allowing for faster print run times. They also have little *show-through*, which occurs when ink printed on one side of the paper or substrate can be seen through the paper on the other side, making the use of thinner substrates more of a possibility. In addition, gravure inks are rub resistant and do not rub off of the finished product. Also, because the ink is transferred directly to the substrate from the gravure cylinder, there is precise color control throughout the press run.

IMAGE AND COLOR QUALITY

Gravure printing is known for its ability to print high-quality images, as well as its ability to achieve intense color with one pass through the press. The engraved cells of varying widths and depths give gravure an extended tonal range, allowing very light highlight dots at 5% to the densest solid blacks. This results in quality often unmatched by other printing processes.

Ink density is also consistent throughout the process and the engraved cylinder can lay down varying ink-film thickness or density when necessary. The engraving of the cylinder controls color as well, allowing millions of impressions to be produced without color variation. This makes gravure a good choice for printing work in which exact color matches are critical, such as catalogs where product colors are displayed.

GRAVURE PRESS CONTROL

Gravure presses are easy to control. Press operations are efficient, with a fast start-up time. It is an economical process with low waste, and requires little manpower.

COST

The main disadvantage of gravure is that it has the highest prepress cost of any of the printing processes. The process of engraving or etching the gravure cylinder, and the cost of the cylinder itself, is quite expensive in comparison to the plates used in other printing processes. Because the cost of cylinder preparation is so high, gravure is more appropriate for longer run lengths, typically in the millions. It is not feasible to spend the money producing gravure cylinders if they are only going to be used for short-run markets.

PRINTING DEFECTS

Like every printing process, gravure has certain printing defects that can occur and may negatively affect your printed design. The gravure press operators typically take care of these problems; just be aware, these problems are common and sometimes go unnoticed, reducing the quality of your design.

- **Skipping** Cell skipping happens when individual cells fail to print because the ink does not transfer from the cells to the substrate. This can result from a rough substrate or a lack of sufficient impression pressure.

- **Mottle (crawl, poor ink lay)** Mottle is an irregular or uneven rippled appearance in solid areas of a design with small light and dark areas. This is typically caused by problems with the viscosity, or the ink's resistance to flow, of the particular ink being used.

- **Drag-out (spill-out)** Drag-out occurs when ink is dragged from an engraved area on the cylinder by debris clinging to the doctor blade.

- **Haze (scumming, fogging)** Haze is an unwanted ink film that appears on the printed design as a result of the doctor blade failing to completely scrape or wipe ink from the non-image areas of the gravure cylinder.

- **Set-off (offset)** Set-off refers to the transfer of ink from a printed sheet to the back of the sheet next to it. This problem is usually caused by incomplete ink drying.

- **Picking** Picking is when partially dried ink or part of the substrate transfers from a substrate web to a cylinder, typically the impression roller. Drying the ink completely will usually eliminate this problem.

- **Pinholing (doughnuts)** Pinholing occurs when the printed ink fails to form a complete film. This often looks like a doughnut where the ink transfers more at the edges of the cells, leaving hollow centers.

- **Railroading (tracks, doctor streaks)** Railroading is the appearance of parallel lines of ink that show up in an unengraved portion of the design. This is usually caused by damage to the engraved cylinder, or because of nicks in the doctor blade.

- **Screening** Screening occurs when ink does not flow evenly among the cells, causing an uneven solid appearing as a screen pattern. This is usually caused by problems with the ink drying too quickly.

- **Snowflaking** Snowflaking is the appearance of random, minute spots of unprinted areas showing through an ink film. These are usually seen in midtones and highlight areas.

- **Volcanoes** Volcanoes are defects that resemble a volcano crater or a bubble, typically found in a heavy-coverage areas of the design. They can be caused by solvent vapors that are trapped under a dried ink film, or by foam in the ink.

- **Whiskering (feathering)** Whiskering occurs when fine hair-like lines appear to be dragged from solid print areas to non-print areas. These are usually a result of paper characteristics, dry atmospheric conditions, and problems with ink and the amount of solvent used.

DESIGN CONSIDERATIONS

TYPE AND LINE ART

Avoid using fine type and line art with gravure. If you use small letters, in particular, serifs, you may sacrifice legibility. Overprinting fine type and line art can be a problem. It is best to use larger lines, no smaller than 0.004 in., and the color that is overprinted should be reduced 30% or less in order to maintain legibility. To maintain legibility and image quality when using reverse type/line art, the thinnest part of the character or rule should not be less than 0.007 in. In addition, you have to consider problems with trapping when using reverse type. Ask your service bureau or printer if trapping is your responsibility. (Trapping is discussed in more detail in Chapter 20.)

CHAPTER 5

DIGITAL PRINTING:
PRINTING WITH PIXELS

Digital printing is one of the current revolutions in the printing business. *Digital printing* is any printing that does not require a plate in order to image a substrate, including electrophotographic inking presses like the Indigo, desktop printers and wide-format inkjet. Digital printing in this chapter refers to commercial-size presses like the Xeikon and the Indigo. Desktop printers are also digital printers, but in this context they are considered proofing devices, not printing presses.

Digital presses use technology that began in the humble copy machine. Lasers are used to "write" the image, and electricity and toner then create the image. Each image printed is a new image, and page sizes vary depending on the press used. Printed jobs go directly from the computer, through the *RIP* (raster image processor, explained in Chapter 23), and begin printing. Some adjustments may need to be made to get the desired effect, but in theory, the first job printed is the final version. This means that the time, materials, and cost associated with other printing processes is much less for digital presses.

HOW DIGITAL PRINTING WORKS

Any printer that goes directly from the computer to print could be considered digital. Usually digital printers do not contain pigment-based inks; they contain dyes, toner, or electrographic inks (as Indigo likes to call them). A few do print with pigment; often these are higher-end proofing devices (discussed in Chapter 19). This chapter covers the non-proofing segment of digital printing: digital presses and large-format inkjet.

Different models of digital printers use different methods to apply the color to the substrate. The two main competitors in the digital press market are Indigo and Xeikon. Xeikon presses are sold by different vendors with different RIP hardware, so these might be called the Xerox DP 50, Agfa Chromapress, or similar devices. The Indigo uses a liquid "ink" that consists of very small toner particles suspended in a liquid, while the Xeikon uses a dry toner technology. There are differences in the printed quality of each method, mainly due to the fact that the Indigo uses pressure to affix the toner to the paper, while the Xeikon uses heat to melt the toner particles into the paper. This results in a gloss effect to Xeikon prints that is not present on Indigo prints. These two digital presses try to duplicate what is possible on a lithography press.

In digital printing, especially with dry toner, paper preparation is very important. The paper has to be the correct temperature and humidity. The Indigo's technology requires the paper to receive a special treatment at the paper mill in order to print correctly. The Xeikon can print on various substrates, they just have to be able to withstand the heat of the fusing unit.

After paper is prepared in the paper supply unit, it travels through the printing engine. Toner is loose powder until it goes through the fusing unit, where it is melted onto the substrate. This creates the glossy effect of toner-based ink. The paper is finally cooled, then cut. While the Indigo uses a different technology, both use electricity rather than plates to transfer the image.

WHAT IS DIGITAL PRINTING USED FOR?

In digital printing, every print can contain new information derived from a computer database. This creates tremendous new design and advertising opportunities. One of the obvious applications of this process are all the personalized mailers from Publishers Clearing House declaring, "You, John Smith, have just won one million dollars." Another possible use of digital printing would be a brochure sent to a regional list of car owners; you have an opportunity to custom design your next car with choices of color, make, features, and so on. If you reply, another mailer is sent with the car you designed and information on how you can order through a local dealer. Most direct mailers have a 1–2% response rate; the kind of mailer just outlined can have up to a 40% response.

Another use for digital printers is to make one or two copies of a book. Some well-known book companies are using this technology to allow them to offer books that are out of print. This costs more than a mass produced book, but when you need an out-of-print book, any price can seem worth it.

When thinking about digital printing, think about customization: customized wallpaper borders, individual copies of books, mailers catering to specific audiences and individuals. Don't think about making a million copies of the same brochure (or even 1,000).

WHY CHOOSE DIGITAL PRINTING OVER LITHOGRAPHY?

- Smaller quantities (1,000 copies or less).

- Quick turnaround is needed.

- To be able to change information quickly, but also quickly get jobs printed on demand. One example would be company manuals — the information may need updating a few times a year. Digital printing allows you to make those changes and then put in frequent, on-demand orders.

- Targeted ad campaign where data will change for each client.

- Printing on uncoated paper. Digital has no dot gain, so the quality is sharper than lithography on uncoated substrates.

- To create a sample version of a book.

WHY CHOOSE LITHOGRAPHY OVER DIGITAL PRINTING?

- Large quantities (1,000 or more).

- Corporate identities. The toner in digital print may melt if a client tries to print a letter on digitally produced letterhead.

- When quality matters more than price. Even if you only have to make 500 annual reports, the quality needs to be excellent. So far, digital does not beat lithography on coated paper stocks.

ADVANTAGES AND DISADVANTAGES OF DIGITAL

CUSTOMIZATION, OR "VARIABLE DATA"
Variable data is the buzzword used by the printing industry to describe the way digital presses handle new information for each page. Each page can contain different names, places, colors, or anything you program into the database.

FLEXIBILITY
Print on demand means jobs between 1 and 1,000 copies can be printed when you need them. There is no need to stockpile thousands of brochures with data that may become obsolete. Keep the template, update as you go, and print as many brochures as you need at a time. This is becoming a standard way to print computer manuals, for example. Location does not matter as much. You can use *distribute-and-print* models, where the job is sent to printers around the country, printed locally, and mailed inexpensively.

Variable Print Length

When web rolls are used in a digital printer, you can print an image that runs the length of the roll if you desire. Because of the digital imaging process, there is no gap on a digital drum as there is in lithography. That means that in digital printing, a wallpaper border can change from beginning to end, thus allowing the entire alphabet on the wall of a child's room. The other print processes are limited by the circumference of the imaging cylinder, which would mean, for example, a child might only see A through E repeated continuously.

Speed and Size

Jobs can be printed in less than an hour. Some digital printers have basic finishing capabilities built in, usually for saddle-stitched booklets. Some can create perfect-bound books. This is a fast way to get a book on demand. Print-on-demand is easy with the digital archiving of files that have already been processed by the RIP, which means that a salesperson can make weekly orders for brochures based on the number she actually needs. It could also mean no more out-of-print books; if a publisher has it on file, you could buy a copy.

For large-volume printing, digital is slow. A litho web press can print 100,000 16-page signatures per hour; a digital press can only manage 10,000 8-page signatures in the same amount of time. Web rolls are still fairly narrow for digital; the current maximum width is around 20 inches. This limits the size of any book signatures, which functionally limits production to saddle-stitching and perfect binding, not sewn binding.

Image Quality

Images do not need super high resolution. In tests done at the Rochester Institute of Technology, there was no visual difference between 300 dpi and 600 dpi documents on a digital press. Even 225–250 dpi is within acceptable visual tolerance, though below that the quality becomes unacceptable. Because you do not need to create film or plates with halftone dots, you can get away with slightly smaller dpi than for other printing processes. The combination of the laser array and the fine toner particles used lets the press achieve, according to the manufacturer, a 170-lpi screen resolution.

Makeready

The transition from a computer to print on a digital press is easy, which is both an advantage and a disadvantage. It means less makeready, but no chance to catch mistakes before trying to print. Since the file goes directly from the computer to printing, there is no time factor for making film, plates, or for running the press until the inks are printing right. You can use the first copy off the press, where lithography often has to build in a 10% waste factor for makeready. If something is wrong with a litho job and it has to be stopped, the down time and new makeready time costs hours; for digital presses, it is a matter of minutes.

DRYING TIME

In Xeikon's technology, the sheet is dry once past the heat fuser. The only exceptions are areas of very dense four-color toner coverage. Printed pages can be bound and shipped immediately after printing is complete.

TONER VS. INK

Most digital presses are trying as hard as they can to duplicate ink on paper (as printed by lithography). In lithography, you have lots of small halftone dots; digital presses have little toner particles. It is physically impossible to get the toner particles as small as the dots of ink. Since the toner particles stick to the paper through static, the particles have to be big enough to not float. The Indigo uses a liquid to suspend the toner particles; they are smaller than with the Xeikon, but still not as small as a lithography dot. Digital presses print with plastic. In lab longevity tests they did as well as inks did, but time will tell how toner holds up compared to ink.

DOT GAIN CONTROL

Digital printing has no dot gain because toner is not pressed into the sheet or absorbed by the substrate. In fact, press operators add in a dot gain value because we are used to seeing dot gain. This shows to greatest advantage when printing on uncoated paper stock. Because of the dot gain involved in lithography, a coarse line screen has to be used, which leads to less image detail. A digital print and a lithographic print, both on uncoated paper, show that the digital looks better. However, lithography still surpasses digital on coated paper stock.

COST

For traditional printing processes that require a substantial makeready investment of time and expense, it is true, "The more you print, the less it costs." Not so for digital printing, where there is no makeready, but no decrease in cost per page either. The cost per page or per book is simply higher than with lithography. The cost of digital printing, however, extends beyond the flat cost of the printed piece. Digital printing saves the expense of throwing away unused materials that can become obsolete before being distributed.

SUBSTRATES

With dry toner, you can print on anything you can stuff through the machine — plastic, wallpaper, coated paper, uncoated, and so on, as long as it doesn't melt in the heater. Papers that do not meet the manufacturer's specs may crack, bubble, and/or resist the toner. Your printer will know the substrates that are best to use; ask if they have any samples. With the Indigo, the paper needs a special treatment and the sheets need to air dry before binding and shipping.

EASE OF PRINTING

The easy transition from computer to print means there is no one to catch mistakes. The job goes from disk to print, and many digital presses do not even have a preview screen. If the job is unprintable, you may be charged for missing the time the printer had budgeted for doing your job. Thus, checking your files before they go to print is a vital part of digital printing. It is also important to talk with the printer before you send the job and make sure you set it up to the paper and other specifications provided.

SHINE

Shine is worse with dry toner than with liquid, where the particles are made of plastic material that has to be melted to bond with the substrate. In the fusing and glossing process, Xeikon prints acquire a distinctive shine.

COLOR GAMUT

While some Indigo presses have six and seven color options, every color requires another revolution of the imaging drum, adding a great deal of time. Most dry-toner based presses are limited to five colors at most. You cannot run extra units of the press, and you cannot run the job through twice, so you are limited to the colors built into the press.

PRINT DEFECTS

Any scratches on the drum mean that those areas can no longer hold the negative charge, and thus end up attracting the toner particles. This can lead to dark lines on every sheet that passes that drum. You may also see blobs of toner if the charge is too low, and speckles of toner instead of smooth fill if the charge is too high.

DESIGN CONSIDERATIONS

COLOR

Check ahead with your digital press operators. Some printers may have trouble printing solid fills of green. That can be problematic with many digital printers, so consider a different background color for your job. In fact, large areas of solid color or screened tints can reflect uneven toner coverage. Screened tints should be used with caution. In some areas of flat color there may be *banding*. It is better to break up a blue sky with clouds, for example. A solid four-color black will usually look fine, but a 50% gray may show gear marks or streaking.

Dark or black type on a colored background may show a halo effect. As the type is applied by one drum in the four-color stack, the electric charge may repel some of the toner particles near the letter. This is a subtle effect inherent in the process.

Heavy toner coverage on the paper may cause it to curl. In addition, toner has a tendency to crack and flake at the fold. Figure out ways to use textured backgrounds, or photographic images instead of solid fills.

PAGE WIDTH

Ask the printer how wide the web roll is. You can design something as long as the length of material on the web roll, but only as wide as the substrate width. You cannot bleed off the edges of the substrate because that would involve loose toner in the machine. Most Indigo printers use sheetfed presses with limited page sizes.

Make sure to leave enough room for the gutter so that your job can be bound. For perfect binding, you need at least a 0.125-in. gutter.

Bottom line, how does printing on a digital press affect your design? The details may not be as fine as with lithography though the result will be close, and on uncoated paper, may even surpass lithography. The colors appear different as well. Dry toner has to be melted to stick to the paper, which causes different colors to take on different glosses. Liquid toner can print smaller particles than dry, and is closer in quality to conventional printing ink. Probably the best way to start designing for toner-based printing would be to look at the portfolio of a digital printer, compare those jobs to similar lithography jobs, and design accordingly.

APPLICATIONS FOR LARGE-FORMAT INKJET

Most inkjet printers are used for proofing and are discussed in the proofing chapter. Large-format printer widths can be over 40 in. wide, and are usually fed from a web roll so various lengths are possible. These large- or wide-format inkjets have created a niche market in recent years, specifically for posters, banners, display units, and proofing.

The resolution capabilities are comparable to desktop inkjets, usually 300–600 dpi. Inkjet printing forces colorants through nozzles onto the paper; most use dyes instead of pigments, since the particles need to be water-soluble. Some inkjet dyes resist moisture and fading, and are suitable for outdoor use. Many large format printers contain six color units — the basic CMYK set, a light tint of cyan, and a light tint of magenta. This allows brighter, more detailed highlights, and less dot gain in the midtones.

Images are rendered in lines that traverse across the substrate. Large flat areas of color can show this banding, and should be avoided.

POSTERS AND BANNERS

Large-format inkjet is great for creating unique banners, posters, and display booth panels. For short-run poster work, this is a better option than screen printing. Substrate choices are broad and include paper, cloth, canvas, backlit film, rigid board, Tyvek, and vinyl. The quality will compare to inkjet proofers like Epson or IRIS.

PROOFING

Wide-format inkjet makes an ideal device for proofing items (such as magazines) that are printed eight pages to a plate. Many of these printers come with high-quality color management programs. You can enter values for the final print, and the computer program attached to the inkjet printer will create a unique set of *lookup values*; from those lookup values you can create a print that mimics the colors of the final press. Some inkjet printers come with double printing units, thus allowing for two-sided proofs, which is ideal when you need to proof something where the front-to-back alignment is critical.

CHAPTER 6

SCREEN PRINTING

Screen printing uses a fine fabric or metal mesh stretched over a frame; ink is pushed through the "screen" with a rubber squeegee.

HOW SCREEN PRINTING WORKS

Once the mesh is stretched across the frame, a photopolymer coating is applied. A film positive is placed on the photopolymer and is then exposed to harden the photopolymer in areas that will not print, or the non-image areas. The unexposed photopolymer, which is the image area, is washed away to create the open areas of the stencil. The screen is then pressed against a substrate and ink is forced through the open areas of the stencil to create the image on the substrate.

Screen printing can be done off-contact, or on a flat surface in which the screen is pressed against the substrate that is placed on a backer board (Figure 6-1). The screen can also be stretched around a cylinder and rotated over the substrate while the ink is pushed through, called cylindrical printing. In addition, screens can be partially wrapped around three-dimensional objects to imprint graphics on manufactured products. Screen printing is the only printing process not restricted to flat substrates.

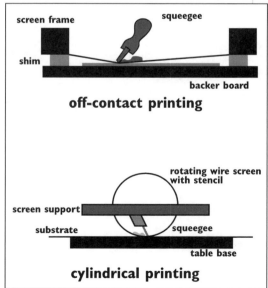

Figure 6-1. Different Screen Printing Methods.

WHAT IS SCREEN PRINTING USED FOR?

Screen printing can be used to print on practically any flat or three-dimensional surface, including paper, plastic, or metal. It is typically used for signage, printed circuit boards, plastic containers, and printed garments. The use of screen printing for large-format signs, however, has been reduced in recent years by the introduction of digital printing. Many screen printers have invested in digital printers to reduce the cost of prepress equipment and material. Digital printing also has a much faster turnaround time than the screen printing process. Screen printing is still widely used for garment printing though, and again, it is the only printing process that can print around three-dimensional objects.

CHAPTER 7

THINKING ABOUT COLOR BEFORE YOU START THE JOB

One of the first things to consider when designing your job is the number of colors you can work with. The number of colors affects how your printed piece will look, and how much it will cost.

Printing presses print color in two ways. *Process color* uses four separate, transparent inks to produce all of the colors you see. Each color is printed using a separate printing plate. The plates print a layer of tiny dots, and the overlapping dots create an illusion of solid color.

If you are printing in full color, you will be using process-color or CMYK inks to produce the colors on your page. This requires at least four printing units on the press, and you have to make sure all of the colors you use in your layout program are CMYK.

The other type of color used in printing is *spot color*, which means one specific ink is used for each color in your design. Spot colors are typically used in jobs that do not have full-color images. For instance, you could design a one-color piece, but choose to use a color other than black; this would be a spot color. You could also print a piece with two or three colors. If you want black text with blue graphics, for example, the blue ink would be a spot color.

Designers often create problems by using spot colors. If you are printing on a four-color press and use a spot color, the press will not be able to print that color. In order to print the extra color, the job would have to run through the press twice. This mistake will cost time and money.

If there are more than four printing units on the press, you can use spot colors in addition to CMYK inks. It is common to see six- or eight-unit printing presses, so the use of spot colors is less of a problem. Printing presses with six or more units allow for hi-fi printing, which adds two or more colors to your job to create a larger color *gamut* — a wider range of colors that can be printed.

PROCESS COLOR GUIDES AND COLOR MATCHING SWATCHES

For scanned images and artwork, it is difficult to specify the exact CMYK values for each individual color. These are usually determined when images are converted to the CMYK color mode. If you want to add a headline, rule, color illustration, or background color, you can specify the color by defining the percentages of the CMYK inks used to create the color.

Most people do not know the exact percentages of CMYK that need to be used. To remedy this problem, you can purchase a commercial process-color guide or color-matching swatches from a company such as Pantone, Trumatch, or Focoltone. You can get these guides directly from the company, your printer, or even at an art store. These guides give you the CMYK values used to create each color, and show you a sample of what they will look like on coated or uncoated paper.

Many software programs also have Pantone or other color libraries available for you to choose from on your computer. Remember, you cannot always trust your monitor. The printed color will most likely look different than it does on screen.

You should check with your printer to find out what type of ink they use before you buy a guide. You do not want to use a color from a Pantone guide if your printer used Trumatch inks. Also, you should be aware that over time, the color guides will change and colors will look different than when they are actually printed. You should try to replace your color swatch books annually.

Once you find a color you would like to use, all you have to do is enter the values into the color picker of your software. To learn how to create process color in software programs, check your user manual.

WHAT IS A SPOT COLOR?

As already stated, a spot color, often referred to as a custom, Pantone, or solid color, is created on press with one ink rather than creating that color by combining cyan, magenta, yellow, and black inks. A spot color is any other single printed color besides black. For instance, if you were designing a book with black text and wanted to add a border or graphic of another color, the other color would be a spot color.

Spot color is a very good option when you want to add some variety to your design but the cost of using process color on a four-color press is prohibitive. A second or even third color can make your design more visually appealing, and can help to add emphasis to certain areas. Your printer will most likely charge you extra for colors other than black, but it should still be cheaper than using process-color printing.

How Spot Colors Were Developed

Spot colors are made by mixing a certain combination of inks. In the past, it was difficult to get the exact combination each time, so spot colors were not always consistent. In 1963, Lawrence Herbert found a solution to this problem. He invented the Pantone Matching System, which identifies each spot color with a specific Pantone color name and/or number and provides the exact ink formula. The Pantone system allows printers to look up specific ink combinations for the color or colors you use in your design. You do not have to worry about achieving consistent color, even if you want to use the same color again in the future, but decide to have your design printed elsewhere.

In addition to Pantone, the *DIC Color System Guide* and *Toyo Color Finder*, mostly used in Japan, are also used for matching spot colors. Like the Pantone process color matching swatches, you can get spot color-matching swatches, such as the *Pantone Color Formula Guide*, directly from the company, your printer, or an art store.

TIP: Toyo and DIC spot color inks are used in Japan. Check with your print shop to see if they can mix these inks before you use them.

All three color-matching systems have libraries that are found in most desktop publishing/page layout programs and allow you to choose the spot color you want to use in your design. Again, the color you choose will most likely look different on your monitor than it does when printed. It is smarter to use the color guides or swatches if you want to know exactly how the color is going to look on paper or other substrate.

You also have the option of asking your printer for an *ink draw-down*, or a sample of the color on the substrate you will be using. Paper has an effect on the appearance of color, so a draw-down could save you from unwanted surprises. It is also important to ask your printer which type of spot color inks they use, or your color may not turn out as you expect.

Why Use a Spot Color?

Company Recognition One important use of spot color is to match a specific color in a company product or logo. Process inks can create yellow, but probably will not match the Kodak yellow exactly.

Colors used for company logos may be specially mixed inks. If you are designing for a company with a specific logo color, make sure you are using the correct spot-color ink. If you are already using process color in your design, you will have to get your job printed with five colors, which will increase the cost. There are, however, books available showing CMYK conversion values for spot colors. You may want to select a logo color where the CMYK values can be acceptable substitutes.

Fluorescent or Metallic Effects Spot colors are also good for creating a special effect in the color of your design. Perhaps you want a specific area to look gold, or you want something to seem like it is glowing. Metallic inks such as silver and gold cannot be created using process inks. Fluorescent colors that seem to glow cannot be created using process inks either; those are inks that have special chemicals added to them. Both metallic and fluorescent colors have to be produced with spot colors, which means more money if you are using them with process inks because they are the fifth, or even sixth, color being printed. If your design needs that, it may be worth the added cost.

Varnish A varnish is a printed coat of shellac or plastic, therefore it cannot be printed using process inks. It is not actually a color, but is designated as a separate spot color. Varnishes are often used to draw attention to a particular area of a design. If it were used on a photograph in the design, the photograph would appear to be very shiny compared to the rest of the page.

NAMING SPOT COLORS

If your design involves the use of various software applications and you are using the same spot color in all programs, then it is necessary that the spot color have the exact same name in all programs. If you choose a spot color from a library in your software or from a guidebook, make sure the number has the same suffix, for example CVC or CVU, because 295 CVC and 295 CVU are not the same. This will create two pieces of film when you or the service bureau creates separations for your design.

Also, if you use a light blue Pantone spot color or create a light blue process color and change the name to "Sky Blue," then you use it in your illustration made in Adobe Illustrator, it must have the same name. If you change the name to "sky blue" you will have a problem. When your final design is separated into film, you will get a separation for "Sky Blue" and a separation for "sky blue."

CHAPTER 8

DEALING WITH PAPER

The papermaking process begins with the debarking of the logs. The logs are then sent through a series of chippers equipped with whirling blades, which break the logs down into smaller and smaller pieces. The tiny fragments are then pressure cooked with chemicals in a large vat, called a *digester*, to separate the fibers. Recovered fibers are often added to the pulp. In the final stage of preparation, the wood pulp is cleaned, refined, bleached, and run through a series of beaters until it is a fine slush. Then fillers and other additives can be mixed in. Paper has a certain amount of filler and non-fibrous additives (including clay, calcium carbonate, and titanium dioxide) that are incorporated into the *slurry* to create brightness and opacity in papers.

When preparation is complete, the slush is pumped onto a fast-moving wire screen where it will start to become a continuous sheet of paper. As water is removed from the forming paper, it is pumped into purifiers where the chemicals and particles are removed before it is returned to a stream or river. The chemicals and particles can be burned to provide additional power for the paper mill.

TIP: To tell quickly how ink or toner will lay on a paper, hold an unprinted piece of paper up to the light. The more variations between opaque and translucent areas, the more mottling you will get.

PAPER CHARACTERISTICS

The interaction between paper and ink is a complex science that people in the industry have been working for years to fully understand. There are a few things you can learn to watch out for when printing on paper, including certain printing defects specific to the paper being used:

- **Show-through** Show-through is when the information printed on one side significantly shows through to the other side, especially with lighter-stock papers (without holding the paper up to a light, of course). Show-through is a serious problem.

- **Mottling** Mottling is the visible non-uniformity in density, gloss, or color of printed ink. It occurs when the paper is not uniformly ink absorbent. Mottling is a obvious blotchy look, and is most visible in areas of large solid color.

- **Caliper** Caliper of a paper is the thickness of a single sheet. You can have two sheets of the same caliper, but with a different basis weight.

There are certain characteristics you know you want even before you begin the job, like high gloss or a very smooth surface. However, what are the trade-offs, if any, of these characteristics? The following chart lists some major paper compromises that are made.

Paper Characteristic	Influence on Substrate
Higher Bond	Reduced fold and tear capabilities
Higher Gloss	Reduced opacity and brightness Smoother surface, increased printability
Higher Smoothness	Reduced opacity, brightness, and strength Increased printability and gloss
Higher Caliper	Reduced gloss and smoothness Poorer printability, improved opacity and brightness

PAPER GRAIN

One of the biggest characteristics of paper is the grain. It is very important in printing and especially in binding. If the job is printed on paper and bound with the grain not running parallel to the book spine, it will cause huge problems. (This is explained in more detail in Chapter 11.)

There are several ways to check the grain direction of paper, the first of which is the folding test. A sheet of paper folds more easily and smoothly when the fold is parallel to the grain. If folded against the grain, the small fiber particles break and make an unsatisfactory fold.

The moisture test can also show grain direction; if moisture is applied to one side of a sheet of paper, it immediately starts to curl in one direction. Expansion is on the cross-grain edge; the curl indicates paper grain direction.

The tear test is when a sheet is torn in longitudinal and transverse directions. The tear pattern will be straight when parallel to the grain, and jagged across the grain.

Finally, the bending test works for paper as well as book binding boards. Boards and thick papers are best tested by bending them in both directions.

One direction offers considerably more resistance than the other. When parallel to the grain direction, the resistance is far less than against the grain.

DIFFERENT PAPER GRADES

Different people group papers into different grades. For the purposes of this book, we divide paper into four basic grades: book, cover, bond, and bristol. *Paper grade* and *paper stock* are used interchangeably. All paper grades have a rating system to indicate quality and brightness. The lower the number, the better the paper is; a paper with a rating of one is far better than paper with a rating of four.

BOOK-GRADE PAPER

This grade of paper covers the widest range of printing papers; it is primarily used for books, magazines, posters, brochures, and folders. There are three types of book grade paper: coated, uncoated, and text.

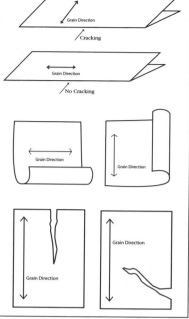

Figure 8-1. Fold Test (top), Moisture Test (middle), and Tear Test (bottom).

Coated papers have different coatings applied, which consist of clay and other materials to give the paper a smoother glossy surface. Some adhesives used for binding do not work well with some coated papers.

Uncoated papers have to be given different surfaces and textures through other processes such as *calendering*. Calendering is when the paper passes through steel rollers to give the paper a certain finish without adding a coating. Uncoated papers have a higher dot gain than coated papers. Colors tend to appear duller on uncoated paper; coatings increase gloss, making colors look more vibrant.

Text paper is mainly used for items like announcements and brochures; both are often available with matching envelopes.

COVER-GRADE PAPER

Cover papers are heavier weights of paper. They are often available with a matching book grade. Cover grades are very stiff due to their weight, and will require scoring before any folding. *Scoring* is a strong impression on the paper to make folding easier. Without scoring, heavy papers such as cover stocks will crack when folded. This grade often includes *Bristol papers*, or heavy-weight papers much like cover stocks, used for greeting cards, menus, paperback book covers, and the like.

TIP: Uncoated papers require you to open up the midtones even more in your images since uncoated paper has a heavier dot gain than coated paper. If you are using a colored paper, you can ask the printer for ink drawdowns, which are ink samples smeared on the paper to see how they react on the colored paper.

BOND-GRADE PAPER

This grade of paper is mainly used for letterhead and business forms. There are two kinds of bond papers, sulphite and cotton fiber.

OTHER GRADE PAPER

This category includes specialty papers and other various substrates like labels and packaging materials.

WATERMARKS

Watermarks have become a new design element in bond-grade papers. At one time, they were mostly used by paper manufacturers to denote a quality paper. They are now used by companies to indicate authenticity and professionalism. A watermark is created during the paper production phase. It passes under a *dandy roll* while the paper is still wet, which creates the watermark by shifting the paper fibers around. There are two kinds of watermarks: raised-wire watermark and shadow watermark.

RAISED-WIRE WATERMARK

This type of watermark looks lighter than the rest of the sheet of paper when held up to light. The image is raised on the dandy roll; paper fibers are pushed away to make the area look lighter.

SHADOW WATERMARK

This type of watermark looks darker than the rest of the sheet of paper. The image is impressed onto the dandy roll and masks the area, which holds in more paper fibers to create a darker effect. Dandy rolls can cost anywhere between $1,500–$15,000. The cost is dependent on the detail of the watermark design. Watermarks are not economical for short runs or tight budgets.

HOW TO READ A SWATCHBOOK

Swatchbooks come in all shapes, sizes, and colors. They are a great reference when choosing the paper for a job. Most swatchbooks have charts listing specific paper availabilities. The following explains how to make sense of those numbers:

Weight and Size Basis 80 lb. Text (25 × 38)	Sheets per Carton	Ultra White
8.5 × 11 - 13.77 M	4000	*
11 × 17 - 27.55 M	2000	
23 × 35 - 119 M	1000	*

The first column refers to the paper dimensions. In this case, the paper is a text-grade paper with a basis weight of 80 pounds for paper cut to 25×38 in. *Basis weight* is the weight (in pounds) of a ream of paper (500 sheets) cut to a standard size. Basis weight is also referred to as *substance* or *ream weight*. The standard size is imperative. Someone cannot just say a paper has a basis weight of 20 pounds without saying the size it was cut from. A paper with a basis weight of 20 pounds cut from a 25×38-in. sheet is very different from a paper with a basis weight of 20 pounds cut from a 30×40-in. sheet.

The next three rows below are the paper sizes available, for example, 11×17 in. The number 17 is bold, which tells the user that the grain of the paper runs parallel to that dimension. Some paper manufacturers may underline the dimension for grain direction. In this case, all the grain directions run along the longer dimension (called *grain long*). If the grain ran parallel to the shorter dimension, it would be called *grain short*. The number with the uppercase M after it indicates its *M-weight*. The M-weight is the weight (in pounds) of 1,000 sheets of paper at the size listed. For example, the weight of 1,000 sheets of this paper at 11×17 in. is 27.55 pounds.

The next two columns are straightforward. The sheets per carton indicate how many sheets of a given size come in a carton. The last column usually lists a color of paper and will indicate whether each size is available in that color. The chart above shows that the 11×17-in. paper is not available in ultra white, but the other two sizes are.

BUYING YOUR PAPER

It is not recommended to buy your own paper and have it delivered to the printer. Printing houses are set up to purchase paper. Printers know how to calculate for paper *spoilage* allowances, which is the amount of paper wasted during makeready and then thrown out or recycled.

If you have a specific paper in mind, let your printer know. They have the resources to locate those papers. Printers also have many *house papers* (often called *house sheets*) available, which are often cheaper because they are papers that the printer already has in stock in large quantities, and therefore can offer at a lower cost.

Not all papers can be used on all presses. The papers used for lithography are not the same ones run through digital printing presses. Some digital presses require that paper be treated with special coatings before it can be run through the press. When selecting a paper for a job, you must consider the printing process being used and the product's end use. You would not run stationery on the same stock you use for business cards. Also, check with the paper manufacturer or your printer about the paper's *runability*, or its ability to be printed without causing problems throughout the printing process.

INTERNATIONAL PAPER SIZES

The rest of the world uses metric units of measurement. If you ever have any contact with printers or clients outside the United States, you will have to know the international (ISO) paper sizes. (ISO sizes are based on a rectangle with a ratio of 1:1.414.)

There are three series of ISO paper sizes: the *A series* is generally used for stationery and publications; the *B series* is used for posters, charts, and other large reproductions; and the *C series* is used for folders, postcards, and envelopes. Within each series, suffix numbers are given, such as A1. The area of each rectangle within a series is half the previous one. For example, the area of B2 is half the area of B1. It is easy to understand by looking at the charts shown here. There are two other series called RA and SRA series, which are used for oversized sheets that allow for bleed when printing, then trimming the excess.

Size	Millimeters
A0	841 × 1189
A1	594 × 841
A2	420 × 594
A3	297 × 420
A4	210 × 297
A5	148 × 210
A6	105 × 148
A7	74 × 105
A8	52 × 74
A9	57 × 52
A10	26 × 37

Size	Millimeters
B0	1000 × 1414
B1	707 × 1000
B2	500 × 707
B3	353 × 500
B4	250 × 353
B5	176 × 250
B6	125 × 176
B7	88 × 125
B8	62 × 88
B9	44 × 62
B10	31 × 44

Size	Millimeters
C0	917 × 1297
C1	648 × 917
C2	458 × 648
C3	324 × 458
C4	229 × 324
C5	162 × 229
C6	114 × 162
C7	81 × 114
C8	57 × 81

Size	Millimeters
RA0	860 × 1220
RA1	610 × 860
RA2	430 × 610
RA3	305 × 430
SRA0	900 × 1280
SRA1	640 × 900
SRA2	450 × 640

CHAPTER 9

LAYOUT AND IMPOSITION: CREATING PRINTABLE LAYOUTS

Once you understand what printers and binders will do to your design, you will be better equipped to deliver a design that prints without problems. When a book goes to print, the pages are rarely printed in consecutive order; the main reason is the need for signatures. The following material explains what signatures are and what is involved in designing with them in mind.

SIGNATURES (CREATING MOCK-UPS)

A *signature* is a large piece of paper that is folded, bound, and trimmed to make the pages of a book. Many books are bound with thread and need a certain thickness of paper layers to sew without ripping the paper. The easiest way to understand how signatures work is to take a piece of paper and fold it in half. That is a 4-page signature; fold it again to create an 8-page signature, and once more to create a 16-page signature.

Note that each 2-page spread has an odd and an even number. A spread is a layout where two pages are printed and trimmed side by side. If you add each pair of page numbers numerically, they add up to seventeen, or one more than the pages in the signature. That remains true no matter how many pages are in the signature. For a 32-page signature, the two pages will add up to 33.

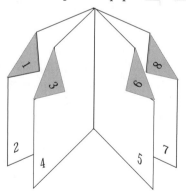

Figure 9-1. An 8-page Signature. After you fold a "dummy," be sure to write the page numbers where they belong (odd numbers always go on the right hand pages). Then take it apart and it should look like an 8-page version of Figure 9-2.

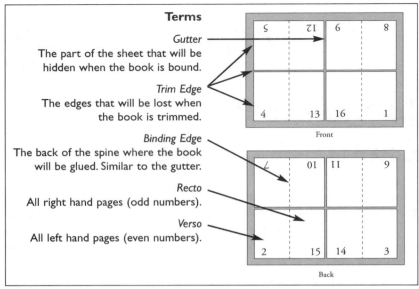

Terms

Gutter
The part of the sheet that will be hidden when the book is bound.

Trim Edge
The edges that will be lost when the book is trimmed.

Binding Edge
The back of the spine where the book will be glued. Similar to the gutter.

Recto
All right hand pages (odd numbers).

Verso
All left hand pages (even numbers).

Front

Back

Figure 9-2. A 16-page Signature Unfolded.

WHERE AND HOW TO PLACE COLOR

Color is another issue in finishing. You can save money if only one side of the sheet is in four-color and the other is in one (remember that black counts as one color). Create a folded and numbered mock-up to explore how to design with color in mind. Take apart booklets at home and check where the four-color spreads are located and how the pages are numbered. It is a good idea to avoid having color that needs to match from one page to the other across a spread unless they are printed on the same press sheet. If not, the ink thickness may shift during the printing process and print different shades on different sections of the print run. A crossover with a large panel of mixed colors may appear different on one side of the fold than the other. In the signature illustrated in Figure 9-2, you could use crossovers that need matching color for the pages 2–3, 14–15, and 10–11. When in doubt, make a dummy and double-check with an expert.

Flattened signature diagrams can be confusing, but as soon as you fold the page into the signature and number it, it all makes sense. Many of the terms here apply whether you are designing a booklet or a full book. Book publishers sometimes use 32- and 64-page signatures, which just adds to the fun. For the most part, you will not need to worry too much about doing the actual imposition. We will address the specific design concerns related to signature imposition in this chapter.

DESIGNING SIGNATURES

DESIGN (READER) SPREADS

Whether described as a *design spread* or as a *reader spread*, this is the format you use when you create the look of the piece. You design with the two-page spread in mind. Obviously, that is how you show it to your client.

The top example in Figure 9-3 is a problem spread. As an abstract design it is fine, but the 1-pt. rule crossing the top of the page, the gradient blend, and the 12-pt. type that crosses the *gutter* (the inside margins) will be problematic when you get to the print and trim stages. The bottom image in Figure 9-3 shows what can happen once the book is perfect bound. The book will not open far enough to see anything in the gutter, and the grinding of the spine will cut part of the image. It is impossible to nail

Figure 9-3. Design (reader) Spreads. These are great for visualizing the finished look, but they do not reflect how the pages will be placed in the book. The bottom image shows what will happen to the printed files.

the registration every time, so the print on the page may jump around slightly. Depending how many vital details need to line up, you can either mask this or focus the viewer's eye on the problems.

Figure 9-4 can survive press variations without as much obvious visual dissonance. The rule is gone and the color is based on a single, solid color, not a four-color hue.

CROSSOVERS

Crossovers are design elements that cross the gutter of a page. The gutter is represented by the dotted line in Figure 9-4 and is the section of the page that will be hidden or destroyed by the binding. Use the following guidelines:

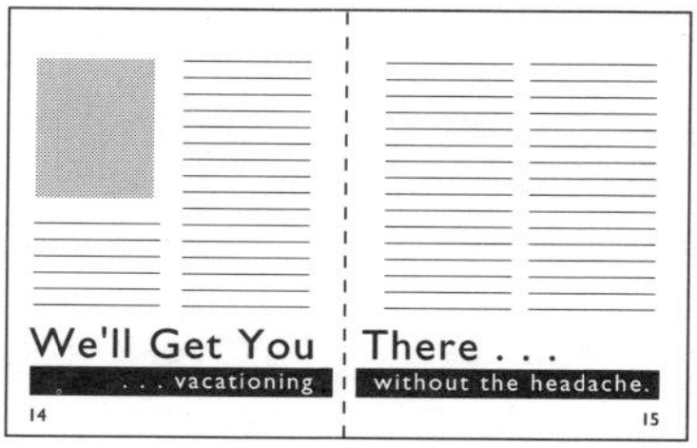

Figure 9-4. Solving the Crossover Problem.

- Never design a crossover photo where important details (like someone's face) are in the center of the spread.

- Avoid tiny type or thin rules that run across the spread.

- Avoid colors that have to match unless the pages will print on the same side of the same press sheet.

- If you need to have a solid color cross the spread, a single color is betters than a four-color build.

Crossover problems are created when a designer fails to account for the gutter of the page. When the printed elements reflect normal press variations, the result can look unprofessional, as occurred in Figure 9-4:

- The smaller type in the lower caption is lost.

- The gradient may not match in hue from one side to the other.

- The larger text size can better mask the loss in the gutter, but chunks of the letter are missing.

- The bleed jumps up from the left page to the right.

- The rule on top jumps up as it goes from left to right.

- The jump in the baseline of the text is not as obvious because the white space helps to mask the jump.

PRINTER SPREADS

Figure 9-5 shows how the job may need to look when it arrives at the printer. Many printers have imposition software that will translate reader spreads to printer spreads, but many do not. Ask ahead. Creating printer spreads involves separating page elements and correctly imposing them for the style of binding you will use. If you want a booklet to be saddle stitched, this is especially important. Definitely, discuss this with your printer before the final hand off; show them your dummy version, and ask for input.

Before you send a job to be printed, you may need to create printer spreads. Each page needs to be printed next to its

Figure 9-5. Printer Spreads.

true opposing page, rather than the way it will look in the end after it is bound. Use your mock-up as your guide and double check with the printer to make sure you are doing it right before you start to create the printer spreads. Find out the dimensions of the printed sheet and use those when you set up spreads in your layout program.

FOLDS

A huge number of folds are possible. As folds get more complex, they will usually require diecutting of some sort. The examples in Figure 9-6 show folds made with the trimmed sheet and no diecut, thus they are cheap and fairly common. Different finishers will have different capabilities. Many copy stores cannot handle a roll fold, for example (not that they are considered a printer or a finisher), while a commercial printer has no problem. If you want to get creative with your folding, do some research into what is possible and economical. Ask your printer if he has pre-made dies available. Many diecut jobs are proprietary, meaning that whoever paid to have the die cast gets exclusive rights to use it.

DESIGN ISSUES

With folded brochures, the key issues are measuring correctly and avoiding cracks on the fold.

- Whatever panels of the brochure are folded first need to be at least 0.125 in. narrower than the outer fold dimensions.

- Create a mock-up version at 100%, then carefully measure the dimensions. (Use a clear printer's ruler that uses picas; it can be easier to remember 21.5 picas instead of 1.85 inches.)

- Measure the front and back of the brochure as separate entities.

- When you design, set up guides that correspond to the measurements of the front and back separately.

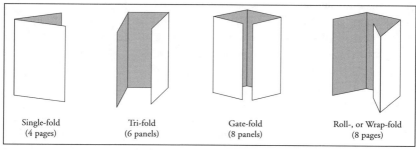

| Single-fold
(4 pages) | Tri-fold
(6 panels) | Gate-fold
(8 panels) | Roll-, or Wrap-fold
(8 pages) |

Figure 9-6. Examples of Common Folds.

- Depending on the paper, ink, and varnish you use, it may be a good idea to avoid having a solid four-color panel that crosses the entire front. It is far too easy to end up cracking the ink as it crosses the fold, especially if it gets printed cross-grain.

DEALING WITH GUTTERS

Creep is the term for the way the inner pages of a signature, or the inner signatures of a saddle-stitched book, stick out from the outer edge of the book block. If you compensate for creep, you should not run into huge problems. Your ideal margins should be used on the middle pages; outer pages will have the printed area closer to the trim edge, and inner pages will have print closer to the binding edge.

If you do not compensate for creep, you may lose some of the inner page's text to the trimmers. The compensation amount will usually not be much more than 0.125 in. (compare the inner margins of a magazine spread in the center and on the outside pages). For a book like a dictionary, signatures might be 64 pages and the creep adjustment is more noticeable. Once the book is trimmed, the outer margins will be all the same, so the only way to evaluate the creep adjustment is by the inner (gutter) margin.

If you do need to compensate for creep, here is a simple method. Create a dummy on the publication-grade paper stock with the correct number of pages. Jog it together by tapping the pages spine down until the inside pages are as far in the booklet as possible. Then measure your gutter and text margins on the front sheet and draw them on with pencil. Keep the pages folded and poke a needle through to the middle of the book at each of the four corners of the text, making sure that you number the pages while it is folded together. When you unfold the dummy signatures, you will have built in creep margins. Connect the dots on your pages and use those margins when you are creating your layout.

Compensating for creep requires knowledge of how the book will be folded, bound, and trimmed. Many printers would rather not have an amateur doing this part of the job. Ask first. If you choose to

folded signature

outer page

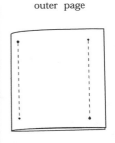

inner page

Figure 9-7. An Easy Way to Compensate for Creep. Computer programs can do this, so check with your service provider before going too far.

do this yourself it may save you some money, but it will take time to learn to do it right. It just may not make sense for you to take this on. If you do, however, compensate; make sure to note this so the printer knows when you give him the job.

CROP AND REGISTRATION MARKS

These marks are printed on the page and trimmed away later. *Registration marks* help the printer to make sure that the four color plates are lining up correctly during printing (*in-register*). The *crop* or *trim marks* show the printer where you want the page to be trimmed. Trim marks need to be set to the final dimension of the book or page. Registration marks are placed automatically when they are selected as an option in the layout program.

Create your final printer spreads on a larger sheet size than the final page dimension. Let's say that your two-page spread was created on a 17×11-in. page to be folded into an 8.5×11-in. book. When setting up to print, select an 18×12-in. sheet size that can accom-

Figure 9-8. Registration and Crop Marks. The little circle with the cross in it is the registration mark; the small lines at the corner are the trim marks.

modate trim and registration marks. Create your printer spreads on the larger sheet, then place in the correct elements from the various pages and save it as a name that will indicate what it is. Again, the prepress department may prefer to handle this, so ask first.

BLEEDS

Bleeds are when portions of an image go past the final edge of the page; an element is said to *bleed off* the page. The black bar in Figure 9-8 is an example of a bleed. Double-check with the printer, but the bleed should usually extend 0.125 in. past the trim edge of the sheet. This is impossible if your original document is the trim size of the design. Once you place the elements into the printer spread, it is easier to extend them past the trim edges to create true bleeds.

As you can see, knowing your final finishing method has a profound impact on how you need to design your job. Chapter 10 discusses printing considerations. With the knowledge from these three chapters, you are off to a great start in creating a printable job.

To Print	Increase Paper size by
Bleed objects	Twice the bleed size for height and width
Crop marks	0.5 in. or 12.7 mm for height and width
Separation names	0.125 in. or 3.2 mm for height
File name and date	0.125 in. or 3.2 mm for height

CHAPTER 10

TIPS FOR DIFFERENT PRINTED PRODUCTS

There are many different printed precuts that can be designed. Each one has its own set of considerations. This chapter lists some of the most common design products and the major considerations for each of them.

PACKAGING

SELECTING FONTS
It is best to use a bold, heavy, or black version of a font. If you choose to swell, frame, or stroke a font to increase its thickness, the *counters* in certain letters may close up. (A counter is the hole in a letter such as o, a, or d.) Smaller point sizes and fonts with fine strokes may not print well, especially if the type is reversed out of a background. Be sure to include your fonts with your file. Even a slightly different version of the same font can cause the type to reflow and throw off your design.

DIECUTS AND SCORES
Make sure you keep important elements of the design, including text and images, away from cuts and scores. If something is too close it may be cut, and the effect of the design will be lost. Consult your printer for the specific die position tolerance of each type.

A die drawing or electronic file must be included with the design to indicate cuts, folds, and scores. You should be provided with a template that includes the layout dimension, non-image area, non-print area, print direction, varnish area, seal area, glue tabs, and so on.

BAR CODES
Bar codes are needed on almost any type of packaging. Ask your printer, or refer to the Accredited Standards Organization for bar code design specifics. There are different types of barcodes; you need to find out which type to use. You also have to be aware of the effect the substrate and color will have on the bar code's scanability. Smoother substrates are more likely to result in bar

codes with accurate spacing of bars; rougher, more textured substrates have a greater chance of resulting in unusable bar codes.

Bar codes should typically have opaque black bars and opaque white backgrounds. Other dark opaque colors such as dark blue, brown, or green can work as well. Red, orange, pink, peach, and yellow can work for the background in addition to white.

Bar code placement in the design is also very important. You should check with the package engineer to make sure the bar code will not be creased, sealed, scored, or folded, all of which can cause problems with the bar code's scanability. The bar code should also be printed parallel to the direction the web is moving so that it is not slurred. Check with your printer to avoid these problems. The size of the bar code depends on various specifications, such as where the package will be scanned. Minimum size requirements must also be met; larger bar codes are recommended.

GRAPHICS AND SCREEN RULING

The screen ruling for packaging will vary depending on the substrate, press width, and so on. Make sure you ask your printer the screen ruling, and select images accordingly. If the printer will be using a low screen ruling, the images you want printed should match that screen rule. Avoid images that have a lower screen rule then the printer you are using; it will only make your photographs and graphics look bad.

MAGAZINES AND PERIODICALS

BLEEDS

If you are going to bleed an image from the page, make sure to extend the image 0.125 in. past the edge or edges you want it to bleed from. If you do not make this allowance, you may end up with white space around the image where you wanted it to bleed as a result of the way the page is trimmed.

BINDING ISSUES

Magazines are typically either saddle-stitched or perfect bound. Make sure you leave appropriate margins for the type of binding that will be used to avoid losing images or text in the gutter.

DIRECT MAIL

TEXT REFLOW

Text that overflows a variable-data text box is a problem specific to variable-data printing. The text overflow may cause unsightly text breaks, or may cause the text to be missing completely. To avoid this problem, designers should create layouts and test them with sample data that has the longest anticipated text string. These layouts should be printed to a PostScript laser printer and proofed to look for possible errors. Designers should make sure they have sample data to work with. Ask the client what the longest and shortest record might be, and test your design with those records.

CHOOSING A SUBSTRATE

Make sure the paper or other substrate you want to use has been approved for use in digital presses. The paper you choose must be able to withstand the high temperatures used to fuse the toner to the paper. Papers that do not meet the press manufacturer's specifications may crack, bubble, resist toner deposit or adhesion, or the toner may flake off the sheet.

POSTERS AND BANNERS

PLACEMENT ISSUES

Indoor posters can have more text and more complexity. It is better to keep outdoor signage simple, unless it will be posted at a bus stop or theater. A billboard, for example, should have one idea expressed in 7–10 words.

REVISITING?

The placement of your poster determines its size, colors, format, number of words, and complexity. Consider the speed of readers on foot, seated, or in a moving vehicle. The faster the audience, the simpler the sign must be.

Will people have time to read the poster? Consider signs on the wall of an escalator, or on the wall of a subway platform. For people in motion, it is better to have a progressive presentation through a series of simple concepts than to repeat a complex poster.

SIZE ISSUES

You are limited by the printing process and the presses available. For example, a screen printing press may come in a 60×100-in. size, or may be 54×144 in. If the printer's specifications say "54-in. material length," then the paper is in some form of web roll instead of precut sheets. This means that you can print a continuous image for a long distance without any plate breaks. Some venues overlap prints to create things like billboards.

SPECIALTY POSTERS

Giclée prints (pronounced jee-clay, French for "sprayed ink") are made with IRIS inkjet technology. These are mostly fine art prints and posters. The main issue to consider is archival quality. Most of these inks are water-based and may fade over time. Some, at least, are pigment-based and, therefore, more able to be archived. Also, you may be able to print on canvas or other unusual substrates.

RANGE OF INKS OR PIGMENTS

Screen printing is the most durable printing. A screen print can have thirty times the density of a litho print, and is often used for keychains, t-shirts, and other hard-use items. Screen printing can also accommodate fluorescent and metallic colorants easily. As usual, ask ahead.

Inkjet printers use water-based inks and may fade over time, but they will have better detail and quality than do screen prints. Some inkjets can now use outdoor, fade-resistant inks.

RANGE OF MATERIALS

Of course posters and banners can be printed on paper, but there are many other substrates available — pretreated canvas, vinyl Tyvek, and others. (Tyvek is the material that Federal Express envelopes are often made of. It is a form of paper/plastic mix that yields a nearly unrippable substrate, and is excellent for durable, lightweight banners.) When printing on canvas, discuss with your printer what you might do to account for the ink absorption of the substrate (dot gain, except that inkjet does not technically use dots). Your printer should have printed samples available to give you and your client a better sense of what to expect.

FINISHING OPTIONS

There are many different finishing options available. Consider the end use of your sign when thinking how it needs to be finished. If it will be carried in a parade, you may want a sewn and looped edge that will allow a pole to slide through the top of the sign. If it will be mounted in a display case, a trimmed edge may be all you need.

- **Trimmed** Trimmed allows for a full bleed. Ask ahead about capabilities; some sizes create trimming problems.

- **Sewn** Sewn means that all the edges of the banner will be hemmed, and is recommended for canvas jobs. Sewing is not an issue for Tyvek because it does not unravel. Signs can also have a loop of extra fabric or paper included at the top during sewing, which allows for insertion of dowel rods for hanging the sign.

- **Grommeted** Grommets in a job mean the edges are usually hemmed and metal eyelets punched through the substrate. This allows for insertion of strings to facilitate hanging the sign.

CORPORATE STATIONERY AND IDENTITY SETS

LOGO DESIGN ISSUES

One of the first things to consider is the kind of color to use. The choice between process color or spot color is an important budgetary decision. For example, a company with two spot colors in its logo will have to print every piece of color printing as a six-color job if they want to match the logo color. Check a swatch book with a comparison chart of spot colors and the process equivalent; you might at least choose a color that is printable as process.

Design logos in vector (Adobe Illustrator, Macromedia FreeHand), not raster (Adobe Photoshop) programs, to accommodate resizing later. A logo will often need to be resized from the size of a postage stamp to the size of a semi truck. That is easily done in a vector program using the scale tool, and image quality is not affected at all. If you design a raster-based (bitmap) logo, you will need to redesign it 10–20 times in every size you might need. Remember that when you send a logo to the Web, you are often sending a rasterized version.

Depending on how broadly your logo will be distributed, you may want to research the meanings of color or shapes in the various cultures your client may be involved. For example, white conveys purity in the United States, but in Korea it means death. Red in the United States might indicate danger, passion, or anger; in China red means happiness and good luck.

BLEEDS

Another decision that will affect the budget is whether to include bleeds. A bleed is anywhere that the color, image, or text extends (intentionally) past the edge of the page. Remember, a *stationery set* usually includes letterhead, envelopes, and business cards; your design should look consistent from one item to the next.

LETTERHEAD

Letterhead is usually an 8.5×11-in. sheet preprinted with a company logo and design, and then used later to print letters. Letterhead with a full bleed looks great, but is expensive. In order to print a bleed, you have to print on paper larger than 8.5×11 and trim it later. Many printers use a page size for printing letterhead that allows them to make three cuts across the printed sheets and have final letter sizes. If you want a bleed, they must have larger sheets and make many more cuts.

If you're going to bleed, don't forget to include trim marks (a black boundary line is a bad idea; it is shown in Figure 10-1 for position only).

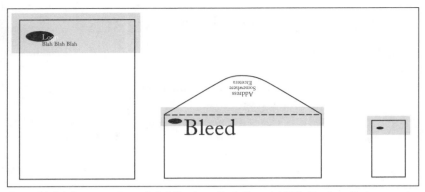

Figure 10-1. A Stationary Set with Full Bleeds on Each Element. While bleeds on business cards are standard, they build in extra cost when letterhead and envelopes are printed.

ENVELOPES

Envelopes come in a range of styles and sizes, and are usually printed on a lighter weight paper. Your service provider should be able to tell you the sizes they can easily accommodate. The Post Office also has rules about envelope sizes, and they give out information kits free on request. The natural assumption is that envelopes are printed first, then cut. However, many times envelopes arrive at the printer pre-assembled and then printed. If that is the case, you can not design a bleed off any of the front edges (not even the top). This also means that printing the address on the envelope flap builds in an extra expense.

If your printer's method is to print on paper, then assemble the envelope after, you will need to work with them to determine what dimensions to use. An unusual envelope dimension will entail the construction of a die in that shape, which is then used to cut the printed paper like a cookie cutter. Ask the printer how much allowance you need to leave, and on which sides, for glue application. If you print all the way to that edge, you will risk white lines showing after the envelopes are folded and glued.

BUSINESS CARDS

A business card is usually 2×3.5 in., printed on heavier card or cover stock. Of the three stationery items, the business card is

Figure 10-2. Business Cards on a Print Sheet with Trim Marks Included.

the only one that you can assume will allow a bleed. These are printed on larger sheets and then cut, since their small size makes it difficult to print any other way. Remember to include trim marks for each item. Figure 10-2 shows an example of a sheet of business cards with trim marks. A bleed usually needs to extend 0.125–0.25 in. past the edge. Trim marks need to be 0.125 in. away from the *live area* (the printed areas).

LITHOGRAPHY VS. DIGITAL

Lithography is preferable to digital presses for printing letterhead and envelopes. The heat used in many desktop printers can melt toner on a digitally printed letterhead.

CREATIVE PRINT FINISHING

Embossing or debossing an identity set can be an elegant design solution. One thing to investigate, though, is at what point a desktop printer may smash an embossed image. You can use engraving inks to print light images on dark paper. It is also possible to lay down an opaque white ink and then print color over it in order to print on colored stock.

TYPE SIZES

Business cards call for smaller type than almost any other form of printed material (except the extensive information sheets that come with pharmaceuticals). Most of the information on a business card is usually set in 8–9 pt. type, with names and titles in 10–12 pt. type.

PAPER ISSUES

While a heavier weight paper conveys an impression of substance and elegance, double-check that it will not jam a printer. Paper suppliers are usually aware of desktop printer issues and can steer you to inkjet-safe papers. But remember that ordering special paper builds in an extra level of cost. Also, just because a paper is shown in a sample book does not mean that it is readily available. Some paper mills wait for an order to come in before they make some of their papers, which means that you have to place a minimum paper order before they will make it. Check with a paper supplier for distinctive but commonly available stock.

For cheaper printing options, obtain the feel of a colored job by using black ink on colored paper stock, vellum, or other unusual substrates; just make sure they are inkjet-safe for desktop printouts. A color stock with two spot inks used in various tints can give a rich feel without the expense. You can also buy duplexed papers in which two different colors of paper are stuck together — one dark, one light.

NEWSPAPER CONSIDERATIONS

While this is a quick overview of some key design issues, consider ordering the SNAP (Specifications for Newsprint Advertising Production) guide for a more in-depth discussion. Newspapers are usually printed on newsprint, which is a low-quality paper grade containing a lot of acidifying agents. This is why newsprint yellows over time. The other distinguishing characteristic is that newsprint soaks up ink like a sponge. Many of the design considerations relate to issues that stem from a newspaper's substrate. The newspaper industry uses a different set of inks than does the magazine industry; magazines use the SWOP default, while newspapers use the SNAP set.

Always include a color proof when sending films or digital files to a newspaper. Since they receive jobs set up for SWOP defaults, they can often account for your proofing methods when trying to match the colors on press. The more information you include about how the image was made, the better: software used, any GCR (*gray component replacement*) compensation, percentage values, curves applied, and so on.

DOT GAIN ISSUES

One of the biggest factors in printing with newsprint is dot gain. While lithographic printing on coated paper commonly sees dot gain in the 20% range (a 50% dot becomes a 70% dot), the range is closer to 30% on newsprint. This means that shadow dots need to be placed around 80% rather than the 95% dot of coated paper, and highlight dots need to be in the 5–15% range instead of the 3–5% range. Confer with your printer to find out the settings they prefer. Remember that tints will look darker than on the monitor or in proofs.

Due to dot gain, sharpening your image before printing is even more important than usual.

SCREEN RULING/LINES PER INCH

Screen rulings for newsprint are in the 85–110 range. If you use a screen rule over 100 lpi, you may need to open up the midtones and three-quartertones. A higher screen ruling means fewer gray levels are possible; as a continuous-tone image gets darker than 50%, it starts down a fast, slippery slope to full black. The fewer gray levels, the faster the journey. The recommended maximum *total area coverage* (TAC) or *total ink limit* for newsprint is 240%. (SWOP is 300%, and many presses allow more.)

LAYOUT ISSUES

Since newspapers are not trimmed, except top and bottom, there are no bleeds. Make the file the actual size for print with no margins. Set up all print options for 100%.

Put all the elements for an ad (logo, photo, graphics, fonts, layout) in one folder. If a logo or graphic is repeated in various ads in the same paper, copy them and include them in the separate ad folders. This is one reason that the newspaper industry likes the idea of a PDF workflow; fewer elements to worry about.

- Flatten copies of your files before sending them to print using the "save as" command. In some software packages, this creates a cleaner, more compact file.
- Use a portrait printing orientation.
- An EPS within another EPS may cause RIP problems.
- Avoid blends that fade to zero.
- Use CMYK (with SNAP ink sets if possible).
- Put registration marks at least 0.25 in. from the live image area.
- Leave a 0.5-in. margin on all sides of the page.
- Watch out for image crossovers.
- Avoid "critical alignments" of 0.125 in. or less.

PROOFING ISSUES

If you proof on coated paper stocks with SWOP or other inks, using SNAP specifications, newspaper dot gain values, and line screens , you will often get flat-looking prints. However, when printed to newsprint, those guidelines mean the difference between a clear, color-balanced image and a muddy, shadow-blocked one.

ANNUAL REPORTS

Annual reports are your chance to push the limits. Most companies go one of two routes: They either design a report that is completely unique and visually daring, or they remain conservative but elegant. There are certain options you can explore (after researching costs and processes), and certain problem areas to remember.

PAPERS

Annual reports often use more than one grade of paper. Many times images and artwork are printed on a different weight and surface texture than the financial figures and other company information.

CREATIVE PRINT FINISHING

Many companies use annual reports to really showcase themselves. Without going overboard, it is an opportunity to be as creative as you can with unique bindings, diecuts, embossing, and foil stamping. For example, one well-known company made their annual report look like a large matchbook, winning several awards for the design.

LAYOUT

With any bound piece, remember to watch your gutters and margins. Do not forget the 0.125-in. bleed and try to avoid any image crossover that does not fall in the center of a book. Make sure you follow all the rules. For example, remember to use tabs when setting up financial charts; odd numbered pages go on the right. Watch out for widows and orphans, and make sure line length is not too long or short. (See Chapter 16 for more on this.)

BOOKS

There are a few considerations unique to book design, involving layout and typeface selection. Odd numbered pages go on the right-hand page; watch out for widows and orphans, and make sure your line length is not too long or too short. Make imposition mockups to check yourself. If the book is imposed in the wrong order, it may not be able to be bound.

Certain typefaces are standard for book design, typically serif faces like Minion, Caslon, and Garamond. Sans serif fonts are harder to read in large amounts. Never lay out book text in a typeface like Impact or a Brush Script.

FORMS

DISTRIBUTION

Distribution is a major consideration with forms. Are they going to be mailed, hand-delivered, or faxed? With faxable forms, avoid small point sizes and light colors. Try making a photocopy of the form; if it is hard to read it will be even worse when faxed. Forms to be mailed have a series of mailing standards to follow, such as size and weight limitations.

LAYOUT

Did you leave enough room for people to write? Create structure for people to write in. Use boxes or alternating color bars with invoices, for example, to help people keep their information organized.

CHAPTER 11

PLANNING FOR FINISHING, BINDING, AND DISTRIBUTION

There are many things to consider before a job is finished. How is it going to be bound? Is creative finishing needed, like embossing or diecutting? How is it going to get where it needs to go? Are there any special distribution considerations that need to be taken care of? The key is to think of the end product, then ask yourself what are all the elements needed to get there.

The fact of the matter is that all these issues need to be addressed in the beginning, when planning a job. They all affect how a job is going to be designed. Talk with the bindery to get specifications that you can use while planning. Remember, each type of binding and finishing technique has its own set of considerations. These are always easier and cheaper to consider *before* a project has begun.

WHICH BINDING METHOD TO CHOOSE

Binding is the way that the pages of a project are put together into one unit. Several factors should be taken into consideration when choosing a binding method — the number of pages, format, type of paper used, paper grain direction, and inserts, to name a few. The easiest thing to do is to speak with the bindery while planning the project.

There are advantages and disadvantages to each binding method. It is important to decide on a method before you start the job because each has specific design considerations and limitations.

SADDLE-STITCHING

Saddle-stitching is the method where pages are folded down the center, which becomes the spine of the booklet, and stapled in that center fold; the finished item is then trimmed on the three outer edges. Saddle-stitching is often used for booklets or calendars.

When a document is too large for saddle-stitching, it can be *side-stitched*, with staples placed about 0.25-in. from the edge. A cover may be glued on. Side-stitched books can not be opened flat and extra allowance is needed in the inner margin.

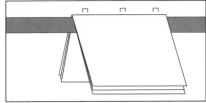

Figure 11-1. Saddle-stitch Binding. Signatures are stacked on a metal bar and run through an automatic stapler, then trimmed on three sides. Many booklets use this method.

ADVANTAGES

- Paper grain direction is not critical if the paper is lightweight. However, it is critical for the cover and any heavyweight papers. Folding against the grain will cause the fold line to crack.

- Paper will not buckle as a result of environmental factors such as humidity. Saddle-stitched items always lay flat, and are ideal for items with images that cross over the gutter.

- It is economical and fast.

DISADVANTAGES

- Saddle-stitching always requires a minimum of four page units. This means that for every one piece of paper you fold in half, you have four sides to print on.

> **CAUTION:** Gutter dimensions are critical. For each type of binding, the dimensions are different. Ask the binder and printer about gutter specifications. If not, you could lose some very important information "in the gutter."

- There are thickness limitations, usually 0.25-in.; otherwise, there are severe creep issues.

- Single cards to be inserted (such as a reply card) must be *tipped in* (glued separately into the pages).

- Saddle-stitched items require a *lap* (edge of the signature) on one side in order for automated machinery to be able to find the center of the item to staple. This means additional paper allowance and waste.

MECHANICAL BINDING

There are two types of mechanical binding: comb, and spiral or coil. Both are often used for presentation booklets because they are quick and easy to make. All forms of mechanical binding allow the document to lay flat when open.

COMB

Pages and covers are perforated with small rectangular holes and a plastic comb strip is inserted through the holes. Comb binding can be used for documents 0.375–2 in. thick.

SPIRAL OR COIL

Small round holes are punched through the edge of the covers and pages, and a plastic or wire coil is threaded through and trimmed to the size of the booklet. This can be incorporated with any size thickness.

Figure 11-2. Mechanical Binding. Anything that uses plastic, metal, etc. to bind the book is considered mechanical. These bindings are great for cookbooks, since they lay perfectly flat and do not need to be propped open.

DOS AND DON'TS FOR MECHANICAL BINDING

- Remember the gutter. You will lose parts of the image to holes in the binding edge.

- Do not place people's faces or any other key areas near the gutter.

- Avoid tiny rules that cross from one page to the next.

- Do not put key text in the gutter; allow at least 0.25–0.5 in. in your design.

TAPE BINDING

Tape binding uses fabric tape with solid glue on one side, which is applied to the edge of the copies, wrapped around, and heated to melt the glue onto the edges of the paper. As the melting takes place, the taping machine applies pressure to wrap the tape around so that it bonds to a portion of the front and back cover sheets. A heavy cloth strip is fused to the edge of the document, which provides a sturdy binding with a neat appearance and allows documents to open flat. It can be used with or without covers, and can support documents 1.5–2 in. thick.

ADHESIVE/PERFECT BINDING

Adhesive/perfect binding is when loose pages or signatures are clamped together, and an adhesive is used to hold them together. Many forms of adhesives and spine preparations are used in adhesive binding. *Spine preparation* refers to the different ways the spine is ground; the spines are filed down in order to expose the paper fibers so that they can be glued. Paperback books are good examples of adhesive binding.

THE STEPS OF ADHESIVE BINDING

1. **Spine Preparation** After all the signatures are gathered together, the spine is ground by a machine. Notches may be cut in the spine. Various methods are used to expose the grain of the paper.

2. **Applying Glue** A layer of adhesive is placed along the spine of the book. The adhesive is able to grip the spine better because of the previous grinding. Different spine preparations and types of glues affect whether the book will be hard or easy to open, and whether the book will stay open unaided.

3. **Applying the Cover** After the glue is added and while it is still wet, the cover sheet is placed over the book block. The glue holds both the book block and the cover.

4. **Trimming** Once the adhesive has set, three sides are trimmed.

Adhesive binding is the number one cause of problems in binding. Adhesive binding is not designed to last forever, and is not meant to be an archival means of binding. There are also many variables which will determine how long the piece will last and how well it will work as a finished piece.

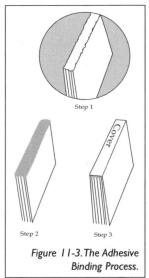

Figure 11-3. The Adhesive Binding Process.

The thickness of the paper affects the *foldability*, which refers to a paper's ability to bend and fold. If a paper is too stiff, it will not lay flat when a book is opened. Think about some of the trade magazines you read. Have you ever noticed certain pages of heavy weight that seem to stand up no matter what, and you have to hold them down when you turn the pages?

Paper strength is a double-edged sword. Paper needs to be flexible enough to keep from cracking when the pages are turned, but needs to be strong enough to withstand the different types of spine preparations.

The key to adhesive binding is in the fibers of the paper. The glue or adhesive needs to form a bond with the paper fibers. The more fibers exposed on the spine, the better the bond will be. Many things will affect the amount of fibers that are exposed.

Grain direction of paper is also critical to adhesive binding; problems will occur if the grain is not parallel to the spine of the book. If a book is printed with the paper grain parallel to the spine, it will open more easily and lay flat. If the binding runs cross-grain, free ends of the paper will swell or shrink but the bound ends will not. The book will then buckle and the binding will weaken. Adhesive-bound books with the wrong grain direction can produce disastrous results.

Many times, however, printers ignore grain direction in order to save money through changes in imposition; the grain of a book's pages is left perpendicular to the spine (also known as *cross-grain.*) Adhesive-bound books with cross-grain bindings will then fall apart. The grain of the paper has been known to be strong enough to rip the book block from the cover. If the *book board* (the hard covers on books) grain runs perpendicular to the book spine, it will cause the boards to buckle. If the *endpaper* grain runs perpendicular to the book spine, it will cause the paper to crease and split. (Endpapers are the sheets that connect the inside cover to the text block.)

Types of Adhesive

Cold emulsion is the first type of adhesive binding. Water in the glue makes it difficult to bind and trim in-line at high speed, even with high-frequency dryers. Nonetheless, because of the water base of both the glue and the paper, it has superior flex and pull strength characteristics.

Perfect binding is a hot-melt adhesive binding. It was developed in an attempt to overcome the disadvantages of cold emulsion, while retaining the desirable characteristics of pull strength and flexibility. Perfect binding with higher-end EVA (hot-melt) glues provide page pulls and flex characteristics equal to cold emulsion. The most important advantage of perfect binding is high speed and relatively low cost.

PUR is a hot-melt adhesive similar to EVA hot melts, but the adhesive is manufactured with polyurethane resins. When the adhesive dries, a natural chemical reaction occurs, which creates a bond superior to ordinary hot melts (sometimes as much as two times the strength). However, one significant disadvantage of PUR is that the books may not be tested for strength for twenty-four hours.

The final category of adhesive binding is *Otabind.* Also known as *lay-flat binding*, the books are gathered, glue is applied to the spine, and the book block is capped covering only the glue. The capping is then side-glued and a cover is applied, adhering only to the side glue, and is detached from the spine. By having the cover detached from the spine, the books lay flatter due to the lack of resistance of the cover glued to the spine of the book.

Advantages

The imposition of the signatures is not critical, since even loose pages can be bound. Adhesive binding creates a spine that can be printed on.

DISADVANTAGES

Grain direction is incredibly important with this form of binding. It will not work if the piece is bound cross-grain. The document to be bound needs to be at least 0.125 in. thick. Depending on the adhesive used, the finished piece may not lie flat. Normal hot melts used in adhesive binding do not recycle and will contaminate recyclable paper waste.

CASE BINDING

Case or *edition binding*, also known as sewn binding or *Smyth sewing*, is the most common type of binding for hardcover books. It involves sewing individual signatures together, flattening the spine, and applying endpapers and a strip of cloth to the spine. The hard covers are then attached. The spine of a casebound hardcover book is typically rounded; there are hinges (grooves) along the edges of the cover near the spine.

Sewn bindings are the most durable, strongest, most flexible, and most expensive bindings available. This method has been used since the Middle Ages, first to sew together vellum (thin animal skins), and later paper. Many books from the sixteenth and seventeenth centuries are still in their original bindings; if a book needs to last, this is the method to use. Textbooks, art books, and collectible books use sewn bindings.

The thread used in case binding is one continuous strand, and is the strength of the book's spine. Needles pierce through the spine of the entire signature and the thread is fed through the holes. After sewing, endpaper is tipped onto the front and back pages of the book block, then glue is applied and a strip of cloth called the *crash* is laid over the spine to add strength. While that dries, the cases (the hard covers) are completed. Thick book boards are covered with cloth, leather, paper, or whatever material is to be the outside of the book. Once that has all dried, the endpaper and cloth strip are glued to the hardcover case. The pages of the book block are held together by the thread, and the book block is held to the hardcover by the endpaper and crash, which are the parts of casebound books that reinforce the binding to make it last longer.

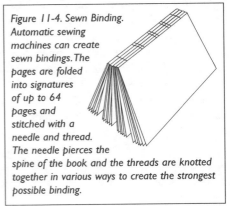

Figure 11-4. Sewn Binding. Automatic sewing machines can create sewn bindings. The pages are folded into signatures of up to 64 pages and stitched with a needle and thread. The needle pierces the spine of the book and the threads are knotted together in various ways to create the strongest possible binding.

Dos and Don'ts for Case Binding

- Use the right number of signatures. The stitching is done by machine; set dimensions will work best, including a set number of signatures. The signatures are fed into a sorting machine before binding; if slots for only twelve signatures exist and you have thirteen, you have designed a job that requires hand binding — a very expensive option.

- Use signatures that are all the same number of pages. Automated sewing machines do not like uneven widths.

- Call the finisher while you are brainstorming the design. Get the phone number from your printer, or call binders in your city. Tell the printer which binder or finisher you will be using. Find out the maximum and minimum number of pages, the maximum and minimum page dimensions you should use, and mistakes you should avoid.

- Make sure the book is printed with the grain parallel to the final fold of the signature.

SPECIAL PROTECTIVE COATINGS

Coatings can protect from fingerprints, scuffing, and any other handling marks. There are two points in the printing process when a coating can be added — during printing (on press), or after printing in the finishing stage.

VARNISH COATINGS

There are two types of varnishes. *Flood varnishes* are applied to the entire sheet; *spot varnishes* are applied to certain areas of a sheet. Varnishes work best on coated papers. They can add shine, color, and protect all in one coat.

AQUEOUS COATINGS

Aqueous coatings are very glossy. They do not scuff or crack easily. They are more expensive than varnishes because a press needs a special coating unit to apply them to a surface.

ULTRAVIOLET COATINGS

This coating offers the highest protection of the three coatings discussed. The coating can be applied during the printing stage or the finishing stage.

WHY USE CREATIVE PRINT FINISHING?

Creative print finishing is truly a mix of science and art. It is not a necessity, but it can add a very interesting visual effect to a piece. Special finishing does cost extra, but by talking with a customer service representative for print finishing, you may find cost-effective ways to execute your ideas.

What Is Diecutting and Scoring?

Diecutting is when a piece calls for an interesting cut-out, one that differs from the normal trim cuts, such as circular cuts or intricate shapes. All packaging uses diecuts to create the shape of the box or package before it is folded. A die is made from steel and mounted to plywood. This is attached to a letterpress after the ink rollers have been removed.

Diecutting uses steel rules to cut shapes from paper and other materials to achieve visual or functional results. Examples include presentation folders, cartons, door hangers, table tents, and telephone or keyboard templates.

Scoring is a strong impression on the paper to make folding easier. Most heavy paper stocks require scoring before they can be folded with a clean, crisp fold. The thicker the paper, the thicker the score impression must be. Scoring stretches the paper fibers along the fold line, so the depth and width of the scoring impression is critical. If the impression is too shallow or narrow, it will fail to make folding easier, or the paper may crack (especially for heavy-weight cover stock).

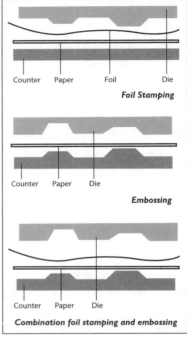

Foil Stamping

Embossing

Combination foil stamping and embossing

Figure 11-5. Creative Print Finishing.

Two Methods of Diecutting *Hollow diecutting* is mostly used for envelopes and labels. The die looks like a cookie cutter, and cuts through a stack of paper using pressure. The pieces cut from the stack remain in the die until they are removed by hand. *Steel rule diecutting* is used for larger dies and projects that need cuts in closer registration.

What Is Foil Stamping?

Foil stamping is also known as *flat stamping*, *hot stamping*, *blocking*, and *leafing*. A piece of colored foil is placed between a piece of paper and a die, which is heated and pressed against the foil and paper. The color layer from the foil is transferred by heat and pressure onto the paper or substrate. The image remains flat; it is not like embossing, which produces a raised image.

Foil stamping can give you an accent in bright metallic colors. In addition, foil stamping comes in other finishes like marble, snake skin, imitation leather, and pearl (which can give an added translucent gloss effect), wood grains, and even holograms.

WHAT IS EMBOSSING?

Embossing is accomplished when an image is pressed into paper using heat and pressure. Paper is pressed between two dies, one with the shape raised (male), the other with the shape recessed (female). This creates a raised image on the page; a recessed image in the page is called *debossing*. There are many different levels of embossing and the pricing is dependent on the complexity of the etching and the design.

Types of Embossing Embossing pushes the paper so that a raised image is formed. Debossing is done using the same process, but the surface is depressed. The following types apply to both embossing and debossing:

- A *blind emboss* is an image that is not stamped over a printed image or with a foil. The color of the image is the same as the paper.

- A *registered emboss* is an embossed image that registers exactly to a printed or foil-stamped image.

- A *combo emboss* refers to an embossed image that is also foil-stamped.

Three Levels of Embossing

- *Single level* — A die that is etched using only one depth level, usually with a single shape, letter, or number. This level of embossing is relatively inexpensive.

- *Multi-level* — For example, a flower might be created using multi-level embossing.

- *Sculptured* — Uses an engraved brass die. It is an expensive and complex form of embossing, but creates a beautiful effect by incorporating different depths and dimensions.

HOW TO DESIGN FOR CREATIVE PRINT FINISHING

Depending on which kind of foil or finish you are using, you may have specific considerations, which you can find out from your service representative. In general, here are the main considerations to incorporate.

Preparing Artwork The emboss should be at least 0.25 in. away from the edge of a sheet to avoid wrinkles and puckers. If the embossing will take place on a finished piece, allow 0.5-in. trim from the edge.

Typography Type to be foil stamped should be no smaller that 8 pt. Remember, the larger the text, the better it works for embossing and foil stamping. Typefaces generally appear bolder when foil stamped. Because of this, be careful of any *kerning* (adjusting the space between letters) and *tracking* (adjusting the space between all letters in a range of type). For type to be foil stamped, try to set more *leading* (the space between lines of type) than you may normally use.

> **TIP:** Tell your finisher what types of papers you plan on using so that they can order the right types of foils, or suggest similar papers that may work better for different processes.

Lines Lines should be at least 2 pt. wide in order to properly work in combination with foil stamping. Areas of fine detail with many intricate lines require special attention. Make sure the area between the lines is no less than half the thickness of the paper you are printing on.

Colors Colored paper stocks in combination with different translucent foils can change the colors you may have intended. Colored papers can also show through foils, changing the look. This occurs more with dark-colored paper stocks. Run tests and talk with your print finishers to avoid some of these problems.

Printers If something like a letterhead has foil stamping, the type of printer used by the client may damage the foil. Laser printers use high temperatures to fuse toner to paper. That temperature may be higher than the tolerance of the foil used in the foil stamp, which can cause the foil to crack, peel, or fall off. It is always a good idea to run a test sheet and check out the effects.

Registration If the design requires tight registration for any type of print finishing, check with the person or company who will be doing the finishing for any production specifications.

Inks When using foil stamping over inked areas, make sure the ink is wax free, and try to avoid UV coatings, which tend to not be able to stamp properly much of the time.

CHOOSING THE RIGHT PAPER FOR CREATIVE FINISHING

The weight of the paper is a special consideration for embossing. If the paper is too thin, embossing will not work as well. The best paper stock to use for embossing is a thick, uncoated stock.

Certain papers, such as vellum, 100% cotton, and other porous papers, will dull some foils.

Recycled papers with a high percentage of recycled materials also create a problem for embossing. They require more pressure to emboss and fine lettering is hard to achieve. Run tests before using recycled stocks for projects involving embossing and foil stamping.

Colored stocks can affect the appearance of foils, especially with translucent and light colored foils.

HOW IS IT GETTING THERE?

When you start a job, you need to consider how it is going to get there, especially if it will be sent through a mail system or other forms of distribution. Envelopes and self-mailers must be designed to comply with certain requirements of the automated system used by the United States Postal Service (USPS). Pieces set up incorrectly will require extra time to be processed and will incur extra charges.

The USPS offers help designing pieces that are going to be sent by mail. They have several free printed publications that explain step-by-step how to design corporate envelopes, different types of reply envelopes, reply cards, postcards, folded mailers, oversized envelopes and more. Just contact your local post office.

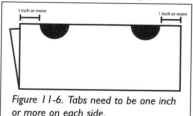

Figure 11-6. Tabs need to be one inch or more on each side.

FOLDED MAILERS

There are many ways to fold a printed piece, and several ways to seal them. Folded mailers must have some sort of seal before going into the mail, preferably circular sticky tabs. These tabs must be at least 1 in. from both sides of the mailer. They must also not interfere with any postal marks that are applied in the distribution process. Address labels can also be used to seal a mailer.

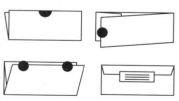

Figure 11-7. Examples of Different Self-mailers.

CHAPTER 12

GETTING FROM A PIXEL
TO A HALFTONE DOT

Some of the frustrations of digital prepress are the many unseen parts of the process that are out of our control. This chapter is designed to give a better sense of what happens in all those hidden stages. Here we are assuming a basic, student, or at-home level of equipment — perhaps a digital camera, a basic desktop scanner, a computer used for storage and manipulation — used to generate a job for an analog printing process (lithography, gravure, flexography, etc.). We further assume the computer will be the intermediary between original work and the printed process, and that the printed process will not be digital (since digital printing does not really use dots).

WHERE DO IMAGES COME FROM?

There are as many sources of images as there are artists creating them: original paintings, prints, photographs, and computer-generated art. For each type of original art, there are difficulties in reproducing it to look just like the original. In fact, the print will contain some compromises for most reproductions; it may mimic the original, but an exact replica is often impossible. As we explore the reproduction process in this chapter, some of the reasons for that will become obvious.

As most fine artists are aware, something is always lost in the transition from an original to a poster or slide. Photographers are also aware of this hazard. Photography often involves reproductions from film to photographic paper (though many photographers today reproduce their work digitally). When black-and-white photographs are reproduced in print, they lose sharpness; blacks are not as dark and there can be less detail in the shadows and highlights. Some of this is an unavoidable consequence of the reproduction process. Even computer-generated art often looks very different from screen to print. The reasons for much of this are related to color realities (as discussed in Chapter 17), and to losses that occur at each stage of the reproduction process.

The first stage of the reproduction process could be considered the grain, or brush-stroke stage. Some original art is created with unique sets of colorants, inks, paints, or tones. Then someone wants to create a poster of that original artwork. Let's trace what happens in order to create that poster.

Before being manipulated on the computer screen, the art has to be digitized. This is the sample stage. There are currently two ways to generate samples of that image — digital photography and scanners.

DIGITAL PHOTOGRAPHY

In digital photography, a picture is taken of the original. Instead of being on a negative, a digital camera consists of channels of red, green, and blue; filters sample out color information into each of those channels. Any point-and-shoot digital camera, even set at high resolution, will have a limited sample size. Higher-end digital cameras have larger information-gathering strips, called area arrays. The more information collected, the more data there is to inform the amount and kind of dot information that will be printed.

There are two kinds of digital cameras, *linear arrays* and *area arrays*. A *linear array* camera works exactly like a scanner, using a single row of sensors to gather color samples. Because of this, these cameras are used for still life studio work where there is no vibration. These are usually very high-end, expensive cameras. The other kind of digital camera is the *area array*, which has a sensor grid that captures the scene in one quick moment. These are generally cheaper than linear array cameras; some of the higher-end versions now rival traditional cameras. The cheaper area array cameras mimic a film speed of 50–150 ASA, which necessitates bright daylight and can expose up to 1/500th of a second. The more expensive cameras mimic 400–800 ASA, which allows for indoor and low-light conditions. The three deficits of area array cameras, particularly cheaper ones, all relate to prepress. These cameras are low resolution, have a low bit depth, and require relatively long exposure times.

Another possibility is purchasing a digital back for a traditional camera, which are also area array systems. One of the things separating bad from good digital cameras is a cooling system. If the sensors in a digital camera overheat, they have trouble "seeing" the shadows, and thus start to add random pixels, particularly in dark areas.

MAKING DIGITAL CAMERAS WORK

To have enough information for printing well, a 3.5×5 in. photo usually needs at least 6 MB of information. Many decent point-and-shoot digital cameras are incapable of the high amount of image capture necessary for reproduction. For a 5×3 in. image, a newspaper reporter might need to capture 1.25 MB, while someone reproducing an image the same dimension for a fine art print might need 3.87 MB of information.

If you use a digital camera, it might be better to use it as a FPO (For Placement Only), then use a film camera, or high-end digital camera for the final version. The final image is best left to a professional photographer.

SCANNERS

Once information from the digital camera is transferred to a disk or computer drive, it is pixel-based information; but while the picture is taken, it is captured through samples. The same is true of a scanner. Both digital cameras and most desktop scanners contain a *charge-coupled device*, or *CCD*. These charge-coupled devices receive light that either bounces off reflective paper or passes through transparent film. Most desktop scanners and digital cameras have what are called *tri-linear arrays*, meaning that the information from the red, green, and blue channels is recorded and stored digitally in one pass.

Figure 12-1 shows three slightly different colored bars on the CCD. Those colors are the filters. The length of the CCD indicates how much information can be sampled. Creating CCDs is expensive; the longer they are, the more expensive. This is a major reason for the price jumps in both digital cameras and scanners. If it is cheap, it will be physically incapable of capturing enough data for printing.

A white light passes over the scanner and light is bounced to a mirror, which bounces the light to the CCD. The red filter only sees information in the cyan range, the green filter sees magenta information, and the blue filter sees yellow.

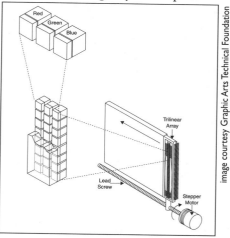

Figure 12-1. A Charge-Coupled Device. The three color bars are actually RGB filters. By having three array devices together, the CCD can capture image data in one pass.

image courtesy Graphic Arts Technical Foundation

Other scanner sensors are complementary metal-oxide semiconductors (CMOS) and photomultiplier tubes (PMT). CMOS are used in some flatbed scanners, and PMT are used exclusively in drum scanners. When saved, the sampled information from a scanner is stored as pixels in the computer.

SCANNER TIPS AND TRICKS

Keep in mind that for higher-quality jobs, a desktop scan may not be enough. A service provider will create a high-resolution version of the image with a drum scanner, and then provide you with a low-resolution version to use for placement. Warm up the scanner for thirty minutes before the first scan.

Put the photos in the center of the scan bed, not on the edges. Most desktop scanners use a lens to focus the sample information onto the sensor. On the edges, some of the information is refracted in order to register on the sensor. The center is a more direct path onto the sensor.

Clean the glass with the proper cloth and cleaning fluid, usually purchased from a camera store; ordinary glass cleaner is not a good idea. *Never* use paper to clean the glass; paper contains wood pulp and is abrasive. You may not notice the microscopic scratches on your windows, but they will show on a scanner. Blow dust off of pictures or negatives with canned compressed air or a blower, also available from a camera store. There are scanners made particularly to scan transparencies (either negatives or positives), which are best to use for scanning film negatives or slides. If possible, wear disposable cotton gloves when handling film. The oils in your fingertips permanently alter the emulsion on film.

Try to scan square to the edge of the scanning bed. Any rotating done in an image manipulation program will soften the image detail. If your scanner is capable of such things, it is best to pick a highlight and shadow dot at the scanning stage. Scan with a grayscale to ensure neutrals, highlights, and shadows; this will save you time at the color reproduction stage. If you are just scanning on a low-end desktop scanner, don't worry about this; it will be done at the service bureau.

SELECTING SCANNER RESOLUTION

Different types of images have different resolution requirements. *Continuous-tone* images (photographs, paintings, etc.) contain a full range of grays or color. *Line art* is usually black-and-white, and includes drawings, graphics, charts, etc. *Graphics* are usually generated in a drawing program like Adobe Illustrator or Macromedia FreeHand, or a program like Microsoft Excel or PowerPoint. Since graphics are usually generated in the computer, they do not need to be scanned.

SCANNING LINE ART

Line art requirements are similar to those of text, which requires very high resolutions to avoid jagged edges. In order to send line art to an imagesetter (a device used to create film separations), you need at least 800 samples per inch and preferably over 1,000. Enlarge it in a photocopier, scan it large, then resize the file in the image manipulation program. You will go from an 8×10-in. drawing at 300 spi to a 2×2.5 at 1200 ppi. Due to the high resolution required, you should save the image with a ppi that uses one-half, one-quarter, or one-eighth the value of the final imagesetter output. For a 2540 laser spot per inch imagesetter, use 655 or 1270 ppi for the final image size.

CONTINUOUS TONE IMAGES

In order to know the best resolution, it helps to have an idea of how you intend to use the image. If it is going on a poster, the image will need to be scanned at a higher resolution than if you just want to print an in-house newsletter. You can create a relatively low-resolution image while you are in the working stages; once you have a better idea of how the photo will be used, you can scan it at the proper resolution. If you will be manipulating the image, you need to use a resolution in the correct ballpark.

Aim for a basic resolution of 300 pixels per inch at 100% reproduction size. Essentially, you need twice whatever line screen you will use. For example, newspaper is printed at 85 lpi so you need a scan of 170 spi in order to provide enough information to generate film or plates for commercial printing. Following are common line screen and resolution ranges:

Newspaper	85-110 lpi	170-220 ppi (can get away with 130–165 ppi, for newspaper only)
Magazine	133-175 lpi	270-350 ppi needed
Annual report	150-200 lpi	300-400 ppi

Line screens are preset amounts; do not pick random numbers within those ranges. Ask your service provider if you need the exact amount. Any less will diminish image quality, while any more may flood your computer and slow down (or stop) the RIP. Here is a helpful formula:

$$SR = OR \times M \times 2$$

- SR = *Scanning Resolution.* The amount of samples per inch needed for the final version.

- OR = *Output Resolution.* The line screen that will be used in creating the printing plates. If you do not know the final output, you could use 150 lpi as a default. (Newspapers use 85 lpi; some high-end annual reports might use 200 lpi. 150 lpi is a ballpark figure.) It is best to check with your service provider to find what they use when printing for film or plates.

- M = *Magnification.* The percentage enlargement from the original. If you scan from a 4×5-in. photograph and you are going to produce an 11×17-in. poster, you would figure out which dimension requires more enlargement. In this case 11 ÷ 4 = 2.75, and 17 ÷ 5 = 3.4. The larger dimension would need to be increased 340%; the magnification factor is 3.4.

If we plug in those numbers:

SR = 150 × 3.4 × 2 = 1020 samples per inch.

That sounds high, but remember that the image will be enlarged a great deal and those pixels of information will be spread out a great deal, which leads to the issue of *resampling*. Once the samples taken by the scanner or digital camera are saved onto the computer, the information is in pixel-per-inch format.

Note:

- A scanner takes samples; the number per inch is considered the *spi* (*samples per inch*).

- The information is stored on the computer in pixels, *ppi* (*pixels per inch*).

- The information is printed in dots, *dpi* (*dots per inch*).

TIP: When asking an illustrator to generate an image, ask if it is possible to generate the image on a flexible media, such as stretched canvas instead of canvas board. This lets you scan the image on a drum scanner, which wraps it around a glass cylinder.

THE PIXEL STAGE

You view pixels on your computer monitor. These picture elements are tiny squares that create a bitmap, which is discussed in detail in the next chapter. A computer is math based; colors for each pixel are indicated by number and changed by mathematic formulas. Of course, you do not see any of the behind-the-scenes math, so you can unwittingly alter the information stored on the computer.

RESAMPLING VS. IMAGE SIZING

When a bitmap image is scanned, it is scanned with a specific number of pixels. When you change the size of the image, you are affecting the pixels themselves by either compressing existing pixels into a smaller space, throwing away extra pixels, or creating new pixels to fill a larger space.

The difference between resampling and changing the image size is the difference between accidentally pixelating your image and merely changing its size without affecting the image information.

If you allow image-editing software to resample the image when you resize it, the computer will use math formulas to figure out what pixel information to throw away, and if you enlarge, what to invent. Once you resample and save an image, that pixel information is forever altered. (This is discussed in Chapter 13.)

THE DOT STAGE

Once the image is in the computer, it needs to be printed. Some desktop printers do not use a PostScript workflow, though many do; imagesetters (laser printers that expose either film or light-sensitive printing plates) always do. In order to generate the printed image, bitmap data has to be rasterized. This happens in the raster image processor before the image is generated on print, film, or plates.

UNDERSTANDING LINES PER INCH, LASER SPOTS, AND HALFTONE DOTS

At this stage lines per inch (lpi) and halftone dots come in. Old mechanical methods of making plates used huge graphic art cameras, filters, and sheets of film. An actual screen with holes was placed in front of high-contrast film to create a halftone screen. Using a large light, they exposed the film with the screen and a transparency version of the original art placed between the film and the light, as shown in Figure 12-2. As you can see, the size of dot created depended on the brightness of the light passing through the transparency. The light areas of the art transparency become the dark area of the film; then, when the film was used to expose a printing plate, it created a light area on the plate. The physical halftone screen was like a window screen but much smaller; it had a certain number of lines per inch. In the traditional method, setting the screen at different angles for each film separation generated screen angles. Today, dot size and screen angle are preset by computer and created by a laser that exposes tiny spots on film.

A coarse screen is used for newspapers, ranging from 85–110 lpi, which creates bigger dots further apart. Uncoated newsprint absorbs a great deal of

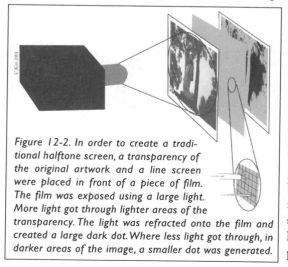

Figure 12-2. In order to create a traditional halftone screen, a transparency of the original artwork and a line screen were placed in front of a piece of film. The film was exposed using a large light. More light got through lighter areas of the transparency. The light was refracted onto the film and created a large dark dot. Where less light got through, in darker areas of the image, a smaller dot was generated.

ink, leading to dot gain. Smaller dots bleed into each other and lose detail. Imagine a watercolor sheet with no water and one with a thin layer of water. If you load a brush with paint and dot the tip of the brush on the dry paper, the dot does not bleed. It even stays raised above the paper surface. If you touch the loaded brush to the wet paper, the color spreads out. If you try to make a bunch of small dots on the wet paper, the paint will just spread further and further; on the dry paper, you can do as many dots as you want. The dry paper approximates coated and/or calendered paper, the wet paper is like newsprint.

In the modern version of dot production, the RIP takes data from the computer and tells a laser when to turn on and off in order to create the dots either on film or a printing plate. This leads to another confusion — new technology generating old output. The laser actually uses thousands of tiny spots per inch to create the halftone dots. A computer generated "line screen" controls the spacing of the dots, though no physical screen is used. Because of this, many new kinds of halftone dots can be used, and new screens, including FM screens, are possible. While the different kinds of dots and screens are interesting, that is an area solidly in the printer's realm.

Figure 12-3 reflects what this means in terms of the numbers used at each stage. The samples per inch (spi) taken by the scanner correspond directly to the pixels per inch (ppi) that you have in the computer. Then, the RIP and the laser in the imagesetter use laser spots per inch (lspi) to generate halftone dots per inch (hdpi). Halftone dots are created with an arbitrary line screen. The lines per inch of the line screen correspond directly to the halftone dots per inch, usually referred to as dots per inch (dpi). The main thing to remember is that in order to give the RIP enough information to create the proper halftone dots, you need to have images with twice the resolution of the line screen that will be used. The highest value practical for lines per inch is around 200. For a newspaper ad, you might only need 200 ppi, where for an annual report that will use a 200 lpi screen, you would need 400 ppi. This is yet another thing to ask your printer before you start scanning.

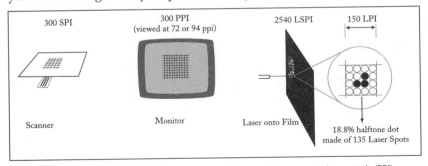

Figure 12-3. The scanner takes samples per inch (SPI), which become pixels per inch (PPI). The RIP controls the laser inside an imagesetter (and/or platesetter), which generates thousands of laser spots per inch (LSPI). These laser spots are spaced apart according to a computer-generated line screen. The lines per inch (LPI) determine how many halftone dots are placed (dots per inch or DPI). The percentage value of the halftone dot, which determines the lightness or darkness of the color in that dot, is determined by what percentage of the cell is occupied by the dot.

The grid of the line screen determine how big a dot can get. That is why the DPI is the same value as the LPI of the screen. The more the dot fills the screen, the higher the dot percentage. The point that most concerns printers is the 50% dot, since that is the place where dot gain shows the most.

Remember that the size of the spots is constant; the number per inch depends on the line screen used. A coarse line screen, like for newsprint, allows for bigger dots (made of the same size spots) spaced further apart. A fine screen, like for lithography, uses smaller dots. The tradeoff is that the number of spots used determines the number of gray levels possible. If you only have 16 spots per cell, you only have 17 possible gray levels.

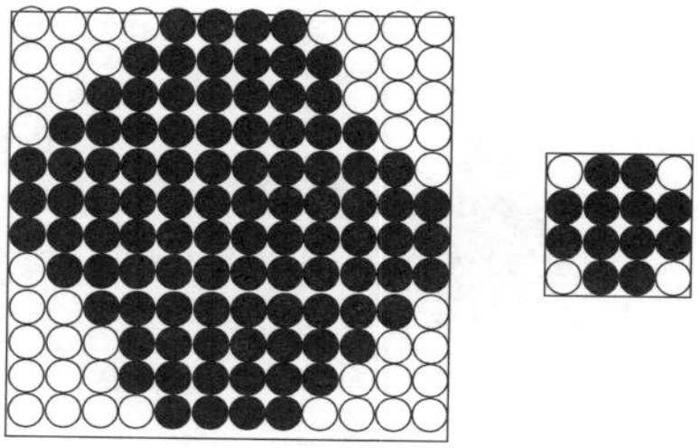

Following is a brief overview of what happens at each stage after the job is on its way to print:

Figure 12-4. Depending on the size of line screen, a larger number of spots will be possible. A coarse screen generates bigger dots farther apart, but many more possible gray levels.

1. **Image to RIP to imagesetter to film** (or Image to RIP to platesetter in a computer-to-plate system) After the image is on film, the film is put over a lithographic plate and exposed under a bright light for a certain amount of time. A different color separation film exposes each plate. For example, Hexachrome uses six films to produce six plates, while process-color uses four films to produce four plates.

2. **Film to plate** After exposure, plates are processed. Lithographic plates are processed chemically; for flexographic plates, light is used to eat away the non-image areas and thus leave raised dots. Gravure plates are etched by a diamond head from computer-based directions; no film is used.

3. **Plate to press** The plate is placed on the press. Whatever necessary inking is done; the plates transfer the image onto the blanket or substrate.

4. **Plate to paper** During the printing stage, there is a lot of pressure between the plates and substrate to make sure the ink transfers properly; this is where dot gain occurs. Each process takes a certain amount of time and energy to fine tune before acceptable prints are produced. Together with how long it takes to create printing plates, this is considered the makeready.

HOW DOES DOT GAIN CONCERN YOU?

There are two kinds of dot gain, mechanical and optical. When the plate is exposed, light scatters a bit and can cause 3–5% *optical dot gain*. During the printing process, the paper and the printing process can cause the ink to spread, thus creating *mechanical dot gain*. Dot gain means the difference between a dark print and an acceptable print.

For the most part, dot gain is the printer's concern. It affects you if you are generating the CMYK versions of your files, and it affects you when you are selecting a paper type. As stated earlier, uncoated paper will have more dot gain than coated paper. For example, if you are using an uncoated paper to print a book (which is frequently the case), you may be limited in your font size. If the font is too small, you could plug up the middle of the letters or lose your serifs. This is a bigger problem if you reverse serif type out of a dark background. During the printing process, the pressure used to transfer from plate to substrate can also generate dot gain. That is why you use the custom CMYK screen to compensate for dot gain.

Dot gain is generally measured at the 50% dot by measuring how much the ink has spread and how big the dot really is. A printer has to measure the amount of dot gain on a certain paper stock, using a certain press, in order to know how much compensation is needed. If a press gains 26% on average, then instead of a 50% dot, the dot will consume 76% of the halftone cell, or line screen per inch. Therefore, before sending the file to press, the dot gain is set to 34%; once it gains, the result is the desired 50% dot. The CMYK settings in Photoshop allow you to input the expected dot gain, and the image is compensated behind the scenes. The GRACoL book contains some common values for dot gain in lithography; FIRST has values for flexography.

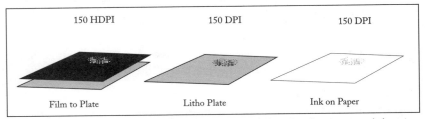

Figure 12-5. There are three places where dot gain occurs. When the plate is exposed, there is a 3–5% optical dot gain. During the impression from plate to paper, there is mechanical dot gain, which is compounded by the paper used. That is why most standards books indicate dot gain values for different substrates.

CHAPTER 13

BITMAP IMAGES

Images that you scan, shoot with a digital camera, or create in programs like Adobe Photoshop are made up of 1s and 0s. This is the language the computer uses to render images. Each 0 or 1 is called a bit; a *bitmap* is an arrangement of all these bits to create an image.

Bitmaps are used in digital images like photographs. Bitmaps are not good for line art or text, which need sharp edges to avoid appearing blurry. Those should be created in vector programs such as Adobe Illustrator or Macromedia FreeHand.

Scaling is another reason to not use a bitmap image. If you have a logo for a company, it needs to be scalable: large enough for a poster one day and small enough for a business card the next. Bitmaps are not scalable without affecting image quality. For line art and logos, it is best to use a vector program.

RESAMPLING AND RESOLUTION

Resampling can be confusing. Think of your image as a checker board. When you change the image size without resampling, the checker squares move closer together or farther apart; all the checkers are there, just in a different order. Figure 13-1 shows what happens to the file size when a 5×7-in. image at 300 ppi is changed to 15×21 in. at 100 ppi without resampling. Note that the file size remains 3.01 MB (1500×2100 pixels). By leaving Resample Image unchecked, the data remains the same, just moving the information around. This can be done as many times as needed without losing data.

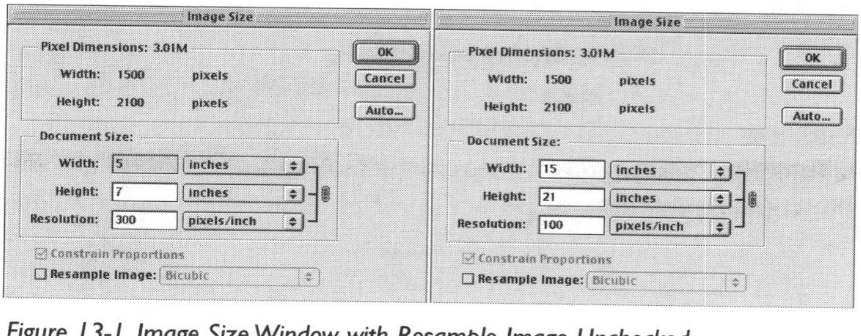

Figure 13-1. Image Size Window with Resample Image Unchecked.

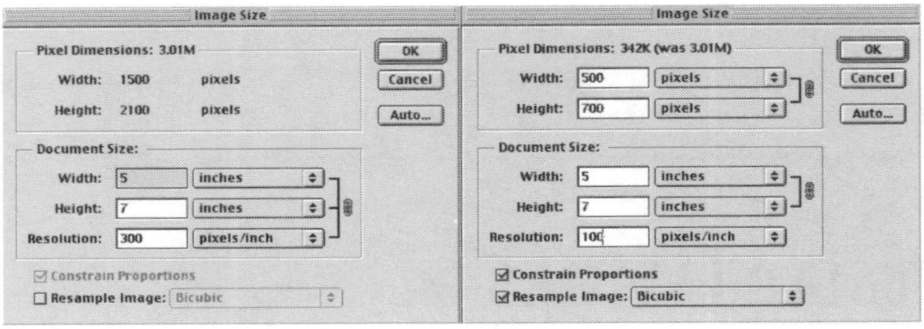

Figure 13-2. Image Size Window with Resample Image Checked.

If the Resample Image box is checked, you are permanently changing pixel information. Referring back to the checker board analogy, resampling actually changes the physical properties of the checker board. Resampling down is like cutting out some of the squares of the checker board; they cannot be retrieved. If you upsample the image, the software actually creates lower-quality clones of existing pixels. This can create large clumps or color that will appear pixilated. Note how the actual pixel dimension changes (Figure 13-2).

WORKING WITH IMAGES

IMAGE MANIPULATION

Any change to an image, even cropping or rotating, needs to be done in a raster or bitmap program such as Adobe Photoshop. If you make those changes in other software, it will cause problems in the RIP and the file may be thrown out. When you manipulate a raster image in any way, the image is changed on a pixel level; if you crop an image in a page layout program for example, the RIP first processes the original raster image and then has to process the changes from the layout program. It is much easier for the RIP to process if the changes have already been made to the original raster image.

CLIPPING PATHS

Clipping paths are another potential problem area for the RIP. Clipping paths outline selections within an image by using anchor points; they can be a designer's best friend or worst enemy. They are great when you have a photograph of a model like the one in Figure 13-3, and you want to place her on a city street corner. There are two methods of creating clipping paths in Photoshop: the magnetic lasso tool, and the pen tool.

Avoid using the lasso tool altogether for this type of work; it provides no real control or editability later. On the other hand, the magnetic lasso tool does give you more control and editability by using anchor points, which can be adjusted at any time. But as you trace the image, this tool will insert countless anchor points.

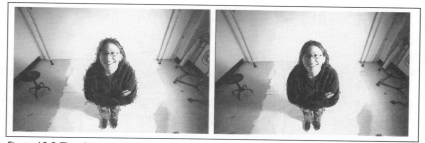

Figure 13-3. The clipping path on the left was created using the magnetic lasso. Notice how many anchor points it has. The same image on the right used the pen tool to create a clipping path, and has fewer anchor points.

There are two major reasons to avoid using the lasso tools. First, the RIP has to process every single one of those points; the more there are, the more the RIP has to process and the longer it takes. The longer a job takes to get to press, the more it can cost and the more chance for something to go wrong. The second reason is that these tools are much harder and more time consuming to control. If you used the magnetic lasso tool to create a clipping path on a job and the client wants a change to the clipping path, you may have to go back and adjust every single one of the many anchor points. Less is more; you are able to get the same accuracy with fewer anchor points.

Use the pen tool to create a clipping path. It gives you the most control, and is the easiest to edit. When saving a file with a clipping path embedded, save the file as an EPS, DCS, or PDF file format.

FLATTENING IMAGES

It is important to know when to flatten an image and when not to. You can create problems by flattening an image too soon. Always keep two versions of each image you work on. Save one that is flattened, which you can use for positioning in a layout program or to make proofs, and save another one that includes all the layers. If you need to go back and make changes, you can open the layered version and save a new flattened version.

ARCHIVING

What happens when you need to go back to an old image or job and change part of it? It can be an easy process or a very difficult one, depending on your archiving system. There are two items to consider when archiving: when to flatten, and when to use the Save As function.

When you are not sure if something is going to work, or if you will like the way it turns out, use Save As. Saving under a different name ensures you do not overwrite your last copy, changing it forever.

SOFT PROOFING AND CHECKING YOUR GAMUT

There are some soft proofing options offered in Adobe Photoshop. Remember, this option changes the monitor display, not the file; it is only effective if the monitor has been properly calibrated.

Another soft proofing option is Gamut Warning, which will reflect what will happen more closely on that printing device. It will mark all the areas of color that the printer description you have selected cannot print. If no printer description is available, a generic CMYK will get you in the ballpark.

SHARPENING IMAGES

When you import an image into Adobe Photoshop, either with a scanner or digital camera, a certain amount of detail is lost in the process. Some sort of sharpening must be done to every image. This only needs to be done once. It doesn't matter if you prefer to sharpen right after the image is imported, or before sending your files to press; the important thing is to remain consistent. Sharpening an image will *not* make an out-of-focus image become in focus. You can only sharpen detail that is there, not detail you want to add. The two main methods for sharpening an image are the Unsharp Mask filter in RGB or CMYK mode, and the Gaussian Blur in L*a*b* mode.

UNSHARP MASK FILTER

Whenever you bring an image into a program like Adobe Photoshop, you should always use the Unsharp Mask filter (Filter>Sharpen> Unsharp Mask). There are three number areas to alter. Many professionals have different sets of numbers that they prefer; leave Radius at 1.2, Threshold between 7 and 10, and adjust the Amount until it is appealing to you.

SHARPENING IN L*A*B* MODE

CIE L*a*b* mode works well for removing noise from digital pictures, and can be used effectively for image sharpening in general. Less expensive digital cameras often produce *visual noise* because the CCDs in such cameras get overheated and start to throw random data into the color channels. This is often worse in the blue channel. Since the LAB space divides into lightness, a* (red to green), and b* (blue to yellow) channels, fixing the blue channel is simple.

CHAPTER 14

VECTOR GRAPHICS

Vector graphics are created with lines and colors that are defined by math. Curves are determined by a series of points and a description of a line's behavior as it passes those points. Dragging handles that are attached to each point on the curve can control their shape. This should sound familiar if you read the chapters on fonts, since this is about beziér curves. Examples of vector (drawing) programs are Adobe Illustrator, Macromedia FreeHand, and CorelDRAW.

WHAT GOOD IS A VECTOR GRAPHIC?

Vector graphics are usually small files; they are not tied to a particular grid structure and can be resized or scaled without detriment to the image quality. A vector program is the ideal place to create graphics, logos, or special-effect text. Particularly for logo design, a vector program is ideal because it permits resizing while a bitmap file does not.

A vector file can contain linked or embedded files, and has some limited capacity to format text, so the temptation is to treat it like a layout program. Many designers seem to feel more comfortable creating pieces like brochures, posters, and other relatively simple pieces in a drawing program. Because vector programs have many options that layout programs do not seem to have, this is understandable. But due to the issues that will be addressed in this chapter, it is better to use the vector program as a place to create special-effect text, logos and other graphic elements, and use a layout program for layout.

POTENTIAL PROBLEMS WITH TEXT

It is better to take the graphic elements into a layout program and do most of the typesetting there. RIPs work better with layout files and layout programs have far more sophisticated text-handling capabilities. In fact, kerning and tracking in a layout program are considered complex elements that can slow down the processing time for your file.

CREATE OUTLINES

You can change text letters to outline shapes by using Type>Create Outlines in Adobe Illustrator, and Text>Convert to Paths in Macromedia FreeHand. This speeds printing since the output device does not have to download the font. When type has been altered or manipulated through fills, transformations, or rotations, you may want to convert to outline. This may change the shape of the letters slightly, so save a copy first. Keep in mind that once you transform the text, you can only edit it as a shape, not as type. Smaller text (12 pt. or under) may gain stroke weight, in which case you may want to embed the font in the EPS file and include it in your fonts folder instead.

LIMIT THE NUMBER OF TYPEFACES USED

One of the principles of design is also a good policy in printing — limit the number of typefaces used in a document. When the RIP processes a file, fonts used in the file must be downloaded in order to be rasterized. The more fonts to download, the longer the RIP time.

LIMIT THE USE OF TYPE ON A PATH

Vector programs give you the ability to make type on a path. This is a great option from a design perspective, but using it to excess can overload the RIP and create printing problems. Converting to outlines may help, but you may want to double-check with your service provider first.

GRADIENTS AND BANDING: THE GOOD, THE BAD, AND THE PRINTABLE

A *gradient* is a fill option for a shape in which color moves from a dark to a light, or from one color to another through a gradual transition. Gradients can be created as linear, moving along a line as they shift tones; as radial, moving from one spot out to a larger circle in a series of circular bands; or as a mesh. There are many different terms used for gradients: vignettes, graduated fills, and blends.

Once you start to learn all that gradients can do, and learn to control the tools, they are wonderful for creating 3D effects, highlights, sunbursts, and all sorts of other options. One of the useful tools in Illustrator is the ability to create gradient meshes, shown in Figure 14-1.

Part of the problem with gradients is that they are easy to use. However, when used for commercial print, a problem called banding may arise. Gradients are created from a series of tiny color bars that extend from one part of the gradient to the other. These bars are supposed to be undetectable, but if the gradient is created incorrectly, the color bars become visible in literal bands that span the gradient.

Certain formulas compute the line screen in order to figure out the number of possible gray levels. The idea is that if you make a gradient within those values, you will not get banding; if your gradient has more degrees of light to dark than the number of gray levels, you may see jumps. If you like formulas, go to the Adobe website and download a FAQ that contains them. Due to the issue of line screens and gray levels, you need a gradient with a greater value shift than the number of gray levels.

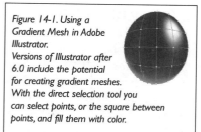

Figure 14-1. Using a Gradient Mesh in Adobe Illustrator.
Versions of Illustrator after 6.0 include the potential for creating gradient meshes. With the direct selection tool you can select points, or the square between points, and fill them with color.

Some tips for gradients:

- Keep gradients under seven inches. The smaller they are, the less noticeable the bands will be.

- The shift in tone should be greater than 50%. The greater the shift, the smaller the tiny color bands and therefore less noticeable.

- Avoid fading to "none" or "white." The last few steps may be more subtle than the printer can handle, and may therefore reveal the banding effect.

- Decrease the lines per inch used in the file. The lower the lpi, the more gray levels possible. The irony to this is that gradients will print better in a newspaper (85-100 lpi) than in an annual report (175-200 lpi).

Remember that banding may not show on your desktop printer, but may on the commercial printer; or it may show on your printer and not on the commercial one. This is an issue to discuss with your service provider to avoid problems on a particular print device.

PATTERNS

Pattern fills are best avoided. It is better to copy and paste an element many times than to use a pattern to fill it. In essence, a pattern falls under the category of an excessive grouping. If you must use a pattern, avoid rotating, scaling, or skewing; it is better to create a pattern at the size and angle it will print. That is why you have to create each corner of a frame pattern rather than just rotating the same one three times.

COLOR MODE AND SPOT COLOR

Because you can change color sliders and import various swatch palettes, vector programs start you thinking loosely about color. The reality, as discussed throughout this book, is that if you are not using the four print colors, you have to designate spot colors. Every swatch you pick will print as a separate plate unless you convert to CMYK. Another option is to do the conversion yourself in the vector program. Note that the color may shift. Swatch books can show you the color as a spot color and what the swatch looks like rendered in just the four process inks.

Composite color means a four-color print of the job. All spot colors are converted to process color and all four channels (cyan, magenta, yellow, black) are printed. A *composite printer* is a printer that only prints composite color prints. You can print separations using the black colorant to render the four color plates, but not specific color separations. Most desktop printers and many proofing devices are composite.

PLACE VS. PASTE: THE LINK ISSUE

It is better to *paste* than to *place*, particularly from one vector graphic program to another. *Placing* creates a linked file, which means you need to keep the original file with the vector program file; *pasting* or *embedding* means that the image data is a permanent part of the file (unless you delete it). There are advantages and disadvantages to linking versus embedding.

ADVANTAGES OF LINKING

- Requires less disk storage space.
- May use less RAM since the file only has to show the preview image.
- Easier to update the file.

DISADVANTAGES OF LINKING

- You must treat the linked file like a layout program and include the original with the job; otherwise, you will print the preview version.
- If you do not choose Preview when saving the original, you may not see the image in either a vector or a layout program (though it will still be there and will print if the link is still there).
- If you do not include the linked file, or if you change the linked file's name or location, the link will be broken.
- Linked images stored on networked servers slow program performance. Copy any files to the desktop and include them in a job folder. It is a good idea to move images into the job folder before placing them in the drawing (or layout) program.

ADVANTAGES TO EMBEDDING

- There is no link to be broken.

DISADVANTAGES OF EMBEDDING

- More disk space may be taken up since you now have two versions of the file (but if you include the original in a separate job folder, that may happen anyway).

- A larger file size.

- RAM needed to display the file increases.

TIP: Do not embed a DCS format in a drawing or layout program; you will lose any spot or varnish channels. Avoid too many complex transformations to a single object. Rotating or transforming a placed bitmap image and then covering it with a complex path will slow printing. The same rules apply here as in layout programs; it is better to resize, crop, and transform in the original program.

TOO MANY POINTS SPOIL THE RIP

COMPLEX PATHS

The fewer points on a line the better. It is easy to put many points to create a shape where only two or three are actually needed. Some automating programs that convert scanned items into vector graphics may put in excess points. The pencil tool will put in far more points than will the pen tool.

Adobe Illustrator contains a tool to Create Compound Paths, which should be used sparingly, since it creates a complex path *and* a grouping. If you are having trouble printing, consider removing any compound paths.

After becoming a compound path, all objects take on the color characteristic of the item furthest back in the grouping. When placed over that object, the other shapes create a transparent shape. A compound path functions as a group. Use the Direct Selection tool to move individual parts and the Move tool to move the group.

SPLIT COMPLEX PATHS

When you print an image with complex paths, one work around is to split complex paths. Try this on a copy of the original file, since it may alter the image. The program arbitrarily puts breaking lines across the image and creates bite-sized chunks for the RIP.

In Adobe Illustrator, you can check the Split Long Paths box in the Document Setup window. The Print window offers an option for splitting complex paths. In Macromedia FreeHand, go to File>Output Options and check the box to split complex paths.

FLATNESS

Curves take longer to process, and require more printer memory than straight lines. When output, curves are actually represented by a series of tiny straight line segments. Flatness causes the curve to join some of those tiny segments to create fewer total segments. Note that in a bitmap program, flatness means to push all the layers into one layer; here it means to flatten out segments of a curve while retaining any layers. If you set flatness too high, you may notice the segments, but some flatness will not hurt and will speed processing time. The user guide will give you an idea of how much to flatten an image. An easy guide is to divide the print device resolution by the output resolution setting. For example, an imagesetter with 2,400 dpi divided by 800 dpi line art equals a flatness of 3.

FreeHand allows you to adjust the flatness level several different ways. In Illustrator, the output resolution (which defaults at 800 dpi) determines the flatness used. A "limit check" error when printing on a PostScript printer means that a complex curve will not print. You can either lower the output resolution through File>Document Set Up, or click the option to Split Long Paths. Be sure to uncheck that box immediately after printing.

EXCESSIVE GROUPING

Try to avoid grouping objects. You can do so while you are using the program, but before your final save, Select All and Ungroup them. Groups of any kind mean that the RIP can not take one shape at a time, requiring it to process the clump together. If there is too much information, the RIP just spits it out.

MASKS AND OTHER WHITE BOXES

It is often easier to cover stray lines or image areas with a white rectangle rather than taking the time to use the scissor tool, or some other means to get rid of extra elements. The result may look fine when proofed to a desktop printer, but before sending the job out you need to clear those areas. What may be invisible to you is visible to the RIP, which must process the information before discarding it. Unfortunately, the hidden areas may print anyway, and the file becomes very slow.

Masks allow the vector program to create these white boxes for you. A mask is basically a program shortcut that creates a white box, or other shape, to hide certain areas of the image. Masks can be a problem due to what is unseen. Use them sparingly, or not at all. If you do have to use one, it is a good idea to keep it simple. Crop the masked item as much as possible and discuss it with your service provider. Delete anything you cannot see in Preview mode. Again, anything on the page, whether you see it or not, has to be processed by the RIP. Even then, some elements may be printed by mistake.

OPEN PATHS

These paths are unfinished, yet filled with a color. The fill may not print, or may print incorrectly.

ILLUSTRATOR AND FREEHAND: A QUICK GLANCE

Illustrator and FreeHand accomplish many of the same tasks, just in different ways. The programmers for Illustrator seem to create tiers of usage. The default screens have the basic options; double clicking on the palette tab, or using the arrow to the right of the palette will often show more advanced options. FreeHand, on the other hand, seems to keep things out in the open. While this clutters the desktop more, it creates a faster learning curve.

The other major difference in the programs is how you select and manipulate objects. FreeHand does not have the Direct Selection tool, though it allows the same functionality. In FreeHand, the same tool does overall moves and individual point adjustment. If you are used to one, the other can be aggravating. FreeHand also builds in more publishing capabilities, which is both good and bad. It is good if you can only afford one program to start with; it is bad because it tempts you to use FreeHand as a layout program. The program can function that way, but it may lead to difficulties in printing.

PREPARING TO PRINT

CROP AND TRIM MARKS

Before sending a job to a service provider, it is a good idea to include crop and trim marks. You can either set up manual marks (a trim line is usually a solid line, and a fold is indicated with a dotted line), or let the program do it for you. In Illustrator, crop marks can be placed in the artwork through Object>Crop Marks>Make. The lines will appear around the document boundary you have set up. If you want to create trim marks for multiple objects on a page (for example, business cards), create a rectangle box in the size you want, then do the same thing. The rectangle will disappear and be replaced by trim marks. It may be easier to create manual trim marks, set them up around the first business card and then copy and paste them onto the sheet, since you can not copy the trim marks. Trim and crop marks should usually be set 0.125–0.25 in. from the object.

CLEAN UP

Before going to print, be sure to delete any stray paths or unused items. Delete unused spot swatches from the swatch palette. Those swatches may create a red flag for a preflight check, even if you never used them. In Illustrator, click on the arrow in the Swatches palette, choose Select All

Unused, and delete. In FreeHand, select the swatch, click on Options, and select Remove. Illustrator also has a Cleanup Command that deletes any stray, unused paths (like clicking with the Type tool, but then never using it). Simply go to Object>Path>Cleanup.

PRINT OPTIONS

Both Illustrator and FreeHand have many printing options. In Illustrator, the options are found under File>Print Setup. You need to access a *Printer Profile Description* (PPD) in your hard drive. Most computers come with default options; you can save a PPD from your service provider in that location.

One key element to note is the box for Convert to Process. Unless you need spot colors, that box should remain checked. By clicking the box to Use Printer's Mark, you enable trim, crop, color bar, and grayscale markings to be printed with the file. These marks will appear around the image area, or the page size, depending on the margins you set below. The page size corresponds to the page size in the print device. Clicking on Overprint Black should print your text over any underlying colors, rather than knocking out, which works well for proofing at home and making sure the right items appear on the right plate. You will end up with a black-and-white print of each plate.

FreeHand has more visible, easy-to-understand options; the screen is just somewhat cluttered. FreeHand features three tabs that control the settings for the print. In the first, click on Print Spot Colors as Process unless you have specific Spot Colors that need to print. If you see a plus sign next to Normal, then the flatness has been set manually through the Imaging Screen. The imaging tab also allows you to select printer's marks, which default to appear around the page size you have in your document setup. Unless you choose a page size in the Paper Setup tab that is larger than the document page, you will not see any printer's marks. You can click the button with three dots to change the PPD. If you click on Separations, but are printing to a composite printer, you will get four black-and-white prints that show the separations. This is a good way to assess spot colors and what is printing on which plate (for example, text should only show up on the black plate). Before using these screens on a job you will be sending to press, check with your service provider for what settings, if any, they would prefer for either program.

CHAPTER 15

Managing Fonts and Type

Problems with type happen because it seems like it should be simple. You assumes the computer is a big typewriter — type it in, and the information is there. Yes, the computer keeps track of which letter you type, but it is up to you to make sure the font and layout stay consistent.

When asking prepress operators which aspect of dealing with designers' files presents the most problems, improper handling of fonts is the common response. This chapter addresses typical font issues and how to avoid them.

The main problems in the printing process center around getting fonts to the RIP and thus to the printer, and in getting the fonts to look as good in print as they looked on your screen (often, even better). First, you need some basic vocabulary.

DEFINING THE TERMS

Previous sections contain the words type, fonts, and RIP. Are fonts and type the same thing? Is R.I.P. what you see on tombstones? Not quite.

- **Typeface** The overall design or look of a font; also called a *face*. Different typefaces are often named for their original designer, even if that specific version is a modern rendition. Bodoni, Garamond, and Jensen are good examples, each of them created and printed with hot-metal type. The digital version of the Adobe Garamond face, for example, was created in 1989.

- **Family of typefaces** The group of faces under the same name in all sizes, postures, and weights. Another term for this is the *alpha-numeric character set*. The Bodoni family includes Bodoni Regular, Bold, Italic, and so on. The Adobe Garamond family would also include the expert set. (An *expert set* contains alternate type characters and aligning numerals, which are addressed in Chapter 16.)

> A typeface is the overall design of a font:
> **Adobe Garamond** and Gill Sans are different faces.
>
> A family can mean any variation of a typeface with the same name.
> i.e., Adobe **Caslon**, *including* The EXPERT SET
> Adobe Caslon Regular 14 point, Bold, Italic, Expert.
>
> A font contains every character in the same size and weight.
> Adobe Caslon Regular, 14 point.

Figure 15-1. An Illustration of Type Definitions.

- **Font** One set of metal type in one size only. 12-pt. Futura Medium would be an example. In today's nomenclature, *font* has become more generic, and is often applied to any set of characters (sometimes called *glyphs*); also, any group of typefaces.

- **Collect fonts for output** Gather all the different sets, from Bodoni to Garamond, that were used in the document.

The other word we will use often in this chapter is RIP. The concept of the RIP, or *Raster Image Processor*, is discussed in detail in Chapter 23. The RIP is a separate computer attached to a specific output device (it could be just a chip inside smaller devices). The RIP's primary task is to make graphic designs (or whatever you want to print) print on the output device. It does this by translating all the colors and fonts in the document into a mechanical language that tells the printer when and where to put ink and when to leave the paper white. It takes time for the RIP to do this translation, and depending on the quality and quantity of information in your document, it can go quickly or slowly or get stuck on things. If the RIP does not find all the information it needs, it may proceed with poor-quality results, or it may *flush* the job (throw the job away without producing anything). Either the service provider can fix it (laboriously and expensively) or they give it back to you to fix. Missing fonts are the number one reason for a flushed job.

KINDS OF FONTS

The reason for incompatible fonts is rooted in the history of innovation. Recently Adobe, Microsoft, and Apple, the main players in font development, got together to create OpenType. OpenType provides one font format that is compatible with Macs and PCs. Until OpenType becomes the accepted standard, each group of fonts is created differently and has different design considerations.

BITMAP

These fonts were in the first computers, and were created to print on the old dot-matrix printers. Most of these fonts have now been made into TrueType versions. If you are using type management, these basic fonts have to be kept in your system folder because they are used to display menu items and other display items used by your computer. The directions in the software package will tell you which ones are needed specifically. The bitmap fonts were mostly given city names: Geneva, New York, and Chicago, to name a few. If you have an old enough system, you may still have some of these in a real bitmap version. If so, your type will be okay at

Figure 15-2. Bitmapped Letters. In a bitmap program like Photoshop, the type can appear jagged along the edges. The G on the left is at 100%; the G on the right was enlarged to 400%.

100%, but when you enlarge, the edges will appear jagged due to the digital construction of the typeface.

POSTSCRIPT/TYPE 1

In the beginning of the computer revolution, two people saw the computer's ability to handle type and images and devised a way to print them out. John Warnock and Charles Geschke founded Adobe, and created fonts that printed smoothly on PostScript print devices; the fonts are known as PostScript or

Type 1 fonts. Warnock and Geschke figured out a programming language called PostScript. The type they created uses *beziér curves* to shape the letters. (Beziér curves are the points with handles on either side of the point. By manipulating the handles, the kind and degree of curve are defined.) PostScript, as a code, tells the printer that from point A to point B, draw a path along a specific line and make it curve according to a specific calculation. For a RIP, this is an easy translation to make.

As a designer, your concern is collecting the pieces of your PostScript fonts for the service provider. With PostScript fonts, two or more elements need to be put in the font folder you provide to the print bureau.

Figure 15-3. PostScript Fonts and Beziér Curves. The curves used in the fonts are composed of points with curve directions built into them. The little handles sticking out from the outline control the angle and amount of the curve.

Figure 15-4. Screen and Printer Fonts. The suitcase at the top contains the screen fonts. If you double-click on it, you should get font previews in various sizes. The other symbols indicate the printer fonts. If you click on them, you will not see anything. However, if they are not there, the font will not print correctly.

PostScript consists of a suitcase containing screen fonts that include *hinting*, which allows your fonts to be viewed clearly on screen. Separate files not in the suitcase consist of an icon with a partial name of the font, which is a clue to help you know that those elements need to go along for the ride to the print provider. If you click on one of those icons, there is nothing to see; that file contains the math formula for that font set. PostScript fonts print well if both pieces are there, and not at all if they are missing.

On a PC, PostScript fonts are identified by an "a" icon. Some of the files are followed by ".pfm" or ".pfb." The .pfm files correspond to the separate icons on the Mac — they are the math formulas for the font. The .pfb files contain the outline that shows on screen. You still need both pieces.

Adobe, of course, has its own set of Type 1 fonts, but other type designers and type foundries have come out with font sets (Monotype, ITC, etc.). These tend to be high-quality fonts that are fairly expensive.

Advantages of PostScript Fonts PostScript fonts are easily enlarged and shrunk, they print beautifully on PostScript print devices (most printers are PostScript devices), and are well designed.

Disadvantages of PostScript Fonts You have to remember to get all the pieces into your font folder, and obtaining a legal version of a PostScript font is expensive. You purchase the right to use the font; you do not actually own the font.

TYPE 3

These fonts are nearly obsolete, but you may run across the term. Type 3 fonts were Adobe's public version, which was missing some of the secret ingredients that made PostScript or Type 1 fonts so well crafted. Today, most of these have been converted to Type 1.

TRUETYPE

TrueType was co-created by Apple and Microsoft in order to break the monopoly PostScript fonts were gaining. The two companies came up with a more complicated system of points and curves called *quadratic curves*. The advantage is that there is only one font suitcase, which contains different sizes and weights of the font. On a Mac, the TrueType font icon has extra versions of the A tucked behind it in the font folder. When you select View>As List, the icon resembles a T. In addition, there is only one font suitcase. A TrueType font on a PC has a .ttf extension and has a "T" on the font file icon.

Figure 15-5. TrueType Fonts.

Advantages of TrueType Fonts Because of the single-folder format, TrueType is easier to transport, with less room to forget the pieces.

Disadvantages of TrueType Fonts Most high-end RIPs do not handle TrueType fonts well. One reason is that the math used in creating the fonts is more complicated and thus slows down the RIP. Many print bureaus will not touch them, and the ones who do will need extra time to work on your job so they can test the fonts. Printers do not like TrueType because the fonts need to be translated into PostScript math before going into the RIP and sometimes the translation is not perfect. This means that the results can be *rasterized* (jaggy) or that the RIP will refuse the font entirely and spit out Courier. Also, the print bureau needs to have a TrueType driver; this is important if you find a font on the Web that you feel strongly about using. Call around to find a printer who is willing to try to print with TrueType.

Most PC computers use TrueType, and most of the fonts that you can download from the Web are TrueType; they are also inexpensive and sometimes free. But it is better to use PostScript or OpenType fonts for design to avoid building in trouble.

OPENTYPE

OpenType combines the strengths of both PostScript and TrueType, and adds even more features. The basic structure is that of TrueType, which means that OpenType has just one suitcase to package with your design job. Adobe contributed the technology to make OpenType compatible with their Postscript printers. One feature of OpenType is its expanded character set that can handle Japanese and Chinese characters. The Adobe web site has an entire PDF document on OpenType for more detailed information.

Advantages of OpenType Fonts The same OpenType typeface works equally well on a PC or Mac. As long as the RIP has updated versions of the print driver, it will be able to handle OpenType. OpenType is compatible with older software. An OpenType font will work in Windows 3.1, though you will not have access to the extended character set. The same font file can handle alternate figures: old-style, small caps, and swashes. OpenType has a compact font structure, so the files are smaller. One bonus of OpenType is that it supposedly gives support for TrueType in PostScript environments; but the printer needs to have the latest Adobe PostScript printer drivers.

Disadvantages of OpenType Fonts Any time a technology is new, there are compatibility issues. OpenType designers worked to minimize these, but the printing industry can be slow to adopt wholesale changes.

Be aware that your print bureau or commercial printer would need to have the latest print drivers in order to print OpenType fonts. For all of OpenType's features (the expanded character sets) to work, you have to have Windows 2000,

> **TIP:** Windows 2000 has Adobe Type Manager (ATM) built in, and OpenType is the native font format. Windows 98 and Windows NT can get OpenType and Type 1 support through ATM Deluxe for Windows or from ATM Lite, which is available at Adobe's web site for free download.

Mac OS 8.6 or higher, and the latest versions of most software. For PC users who do not have Windows 2000, you can use OpenType if you purchase the Adobe Type Manager program. The theory is that this will end up being the only player on the field, minimizing problems, but the industry is not there yet. Avoid assuming; ask your print provider if they can handle OpenType.

MULTIPLE MASTERS

Multiple masters are not different font sets; they are base fonts that contain a "master" version of a typeface. A multiple master lets you alter the weight and dimensions of the face. After you alter the face, it is vital to include the master font in your font folder. The altered face needs the master face as a reference tool.

Multiple Masters can work for logo design, a few headlines, and so on, but should not be used for text type. Only use a multiple master if you plan to create an outline in your drawing program before putting it in a layout program. If you have to send a Multiple Master that you've altered, test it first. Make sure you include the base font in your font folder.

PROBLEMS WITH FONTS

It would seem reasonable to expect that if it prints on your desktop printer, it will print just as well on a commercial press. The following are important reasons that this is not the case.

1. All the fonts you used in your document are stored on *your* computer, that is why it is critical to provide the fonts along with your document; they may not be stored on the computer at the print provider.

2. Some fonts, like TrueType, require a particular RIP to translate more complicated math than others. Others, such as those from an inexpensive CD of thousands of fonts, do not have enough information for the RIP, which can result in the RIP substituting Courier.

3. Remember, the same name does not mean the same typeface; PC Garamond is not Mac Garamond, and Adobe Garamond is not ITC Garamond. If names match exactly, you have a chance that the fonts might be close enough to substitute, but there are different editions of fonts with the same name. PC fonts do not work on Macs and Mac fonts do not work on PCs. You can buy Type 1 or TrueType fonts for either platform, but they will not cross. Only OpenType attempts to be cross-platform.

Figure 15-6. Garamond Comparison. The Mac and PC versions of Adobe Garamond are very close. However, the TrueType version is more rounded. The "o" is close to round vs. the oval shape of the Adobe version.

4. Words or letters "rasterized" in an Adobe Photoshop document may look fuzzy or jagged after being RIPed. This effect worsens when you change the size of the image after rasterizing the type layer. Because of this, it is better to have vector-based type until you know the final size and resolution needed for the layout program. In order to put a Photoshop image into QuarkXPress, it needs to be in TIFF or EPS format, which means flattening it. Be sure to save two versions of the file, a layered version (.psd), as well as the flattened version for export to the layout program.

5. Your desktop printer may not even have a RIP, and if it has one, it might be small and limited. Desktop printers have software-based RIPs. When you realize that a high-end RIP requires a full-size computer to work, you will see there is little comparison between that and a desktop RIP. An Epson only needs enough information to print 600 dots in a 1-in. area; a high-end RIP needs information for over 2,000 dpi. The RIPs for lithographic presses and other high-end print processes are very picky.

FONTS IN BITMAP, VECTOR, AND LAYOUT PROGRAMS

If you have not done so yet, it will help if you read Chapters 13 and 14, since the terms in those chapters will be addressed in this section.

BITMAP PROGRAMS

One of the features of Adobe Photoshop is that the type layers are actually vector layers. You can edit the type, blow it up, shrink it, and it still looks good. The font is not embedded until you rasterize the layer.

DRAWING PROGRAMS

The main thing to remember in drawing programs is that .eps is not the same as does not equal an automatically embedded font. You have three options:

- Put a copy of the font in a folder that you include with your job.

- Click the Embed all Fonts option in the EPS Save window.

- Convert to outlines before going to your layout program.

Creating Outlines If a typeface is used in a graphic, you can create outlines before saving and avoid having to send a copy of the font. In Illustrator select Type>Create Outlines; in FreeHand select Text>Convert to Paths.

Either option just turns the fonts' Bézier or quadratic curves into Postscript outlines. With some artistic fonts, where the font looks like

NOTE: When we say to outline type before importing it into the layout program, we generally mean anything above 14 pt. It is usually not a good idea to outline a body of text 12 pt. or smaller. The better option is to include the font in the font folder inside your desktop job folder. Use Create Outlines for headlines or logotypes.

paint spatters, for instance, this can lead to a ridiculous number of points in the outline. Use your judgment. For example, if the letter "o" has more than 25 points after converting, you may be better off embedding the font and putting a copy in the font folder.

Multiple Master and TrueType fonts will both benefit from Convert to Paths. Multiple Master fonts often have trouble printing, but once converted to outline, the RIP treats them as just another graphic. The same is true of TrueType fonts. If you know that your printer cannot handle these fonts, but you must have TrueType in your graphic, convert to outlines.

LAYOUT PROGRAMS

The aesthetics of dealing with fonts in layout are covered in the next chapter. For now, the important part is that you include all the fonts you use in a font folder that stays with your design.

Keyboard Shortcuts In many word processing and layout programs, there are keyboard shortcuts, or menu options to make type bold, italic, small caps, and so on. Do not use them. If you do not use the actual font (i.e., Garamond Bold), you may get a font substitution in the printed version. There is more on this in the next chapter.

WHAT "COLLECT FOR OUTPUT" DOES AND DOES NOT DO

Every font you use needs to go in a font folder that is kept in your project folder. Every time, without exception, make a folder. As already discussed, if you create a graphic in a drawing program and save it as an EPS file, it *does not embed* the font. You need to either Create Outlines before putting it in the layout, or include the font in your project font folder. Be sure to copy the whole font suitcase; do not open it and copy the contents. You need both elements, the suitcase and its contents.

PDF

If you create a PDF, make sure to embed your fonts. If you do not embed fonts, Acrobat Reader on the recipient's computer will take the PDF description of the kind of font, the size, number of characters per line, etc., and will search the recipient's computer to make an intelligent substitution. This is covered in detail in Chapter 21.

USING A FONT MANAGEMENT PROGRAM EFFECTIVELY

If you have more than twenty fonts in your system's font folder, you have too many. A large number of active fonts slow down your computer, gobble up memory space, and often cause programs to crash or give you error messages.

There are many different font management programs out there. This book refers to Adobe Type Manager (ATM), but other programs have their own strengths. DiamondSoft Font Reserve has a number of great features for sorting and managing fonts, and Extensis Suitcase is also very popular. All of these allow you to move the fonts out of your system folder.

Once you install ATM, you will want to create a folder for your fonts located on your hard drive, but outside of your system folder. The fonts are not stored in the font management program, just managed by it. You leave a basic set in the system folder.

The main idea behind a type management program is to only activate the fonts that are actually in use at any given point. You can also use this as a way to organize your fonts by project. You can copy fonts from their original location into a fonts folder; then it is easy to just copy the whole folder and run. It is also easy for people to temporarily place a font folder on your computer and vice versa. Just copy the font folder from your storage disk onto the desktop, and then drag-and-drop the folder into ATM. It is a bit more complicated on a PC; you have to use the Add Fonts window inside ATM, open the desktop folder from there, select the fonts, then drag them to the "new folder" in the sets window. Name it appropriately, and done.

There are many font programs available for purchase or free download that may make your life easier. For example, FontSneak collects every font used in a document, including the ones in EPS files. Font Gander helps create type sample pages so that you can make your own type style manual. Try going to the Internet and searching under "font," "font aids," "font collection," and so on. Many programs are available for free download.

WARNING ON LEGAL ISSUES

The catch to all your font folders is that, unless your print provider has a license for the fonts you are sending, it is illegal to distribute the font. You purchase the right to use the font, not the right to distribute it. Luckily, most printers and service bureaus either already have or can get licenses cheap from the font creators. If you are using an unusual font, give the print house time to get the license. Most print providers already have a license for the Adobe Type Library, the Monotype Library, and the other major foundries. Just ask. There are substantial fines for illegal distribution of fonts to ensure royalties for the considerable work involved in designing them.

CHAPTER 16

DOS AND DON'TS OF TYPOGRAPHY

As an artist or designer, your job is to use type to create something that is visually appealing. In that case, it is important to remember the specific dos and don'ts of typography.

It is also important to know that the graphic arts industry uses units of measure such as picas and points to describe typography. These are strictly American terms of measure; in Europe, designers use the cicero. Points refer to the height of a typeface, 12-pt. type for example. Picas refer to the width of a line of type, a line length of 22 picas for example.

Inches	Points	Picas
1 inch	72 points	6 picas

USING TYPESETTING BASICS

Figure 16-1 illustrates the major parts of letterforms. Knowing the different parts of a letter will help you recognize the difference between typefaces.

LINE LENGTH AND POINT SIZE

It is important for a body of text, such as a book, magazine article, or newspaper column to be the right length and size for the job. If a piece of text does not have the correct proportion of point size to line length, it becomes hard to follow, and you will lose the reader.

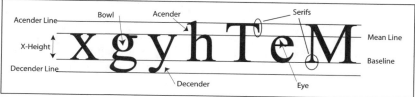

Figure 16-1. The Anatomy of Type.

That come to pass; ere the Pequod's weedy hull rolls side by side with the barnacled hulls of the leviathan; at the outset it is but well to attend to a matter almost indispensable to a thorough appreciative understanding of the more special leviathanic revelations and allusions of all sorts which are to follow.

That come to pass; ere the Pequod's weedy hull rolls side by side with the barnacled hulls of the leviathan; at the outset it is but well to attend to a matter almost indispensable to a thorough appreciative understanding of the more special leviathanic revelations and allusions of all sorts which are to follow.

That come to pass; ere the Pequod's weedy hull rolls side by side with the barnacled hulls of the leviathan; at the outset it is but well to attend to a matter almost indispensable to a thorough appreciative understanding of the more special leviathanic revelations and allusions of all sorts which are to follow.

Figure 16-2. Examples of Different Line Length.

Look at the examples in Figure 16-2. Which one is the easiest to read? If you said the one in the middle, you are correct. *Line length* is the length of a line measured in picas to achieve maximum readability. To calculate the correct line length for a job you are doing, several methods can be followed:

- Twice the point size of the type equals the maximum line length. If you subtract two from that number, you get the optimum line length. For example, 12-pt. text uses a line length of 22 to 24 picas.

- Physically type the complete lowercase alphabet of a given font one and a half times. In other words, type A–Z and then A–M for the specific font using no spaces. The length of the type is your line length, so make your text box that same width.

As line length increases, paragraph indentations should too. Columns are one method for breaking up text to avoid long line length. Think about a newspaper, and how hard it would be to read the news if there were no columns and the text just stretched the whole width of the paper. Who would want to read it? When broken into columns, your eye only has to make minimal movements. The eye is more comfortable reading shorter lines.

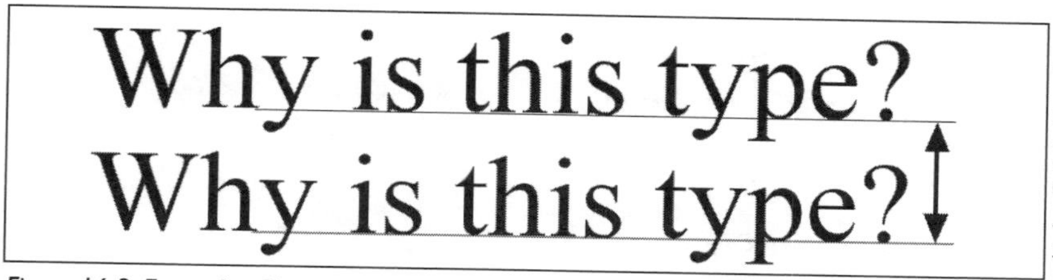

Why is this type?
Why is this type?

Figure 16-3. Example of Line Spacing.

courtesy Graphic Arts Technical Foundation

LINE SPACING

Line spacing, also known as *leading*, is the space between lines of type, measured from baseline to baseline. It refers to the days when metal type was set by hand and pieces of lead were inserted between the lines of type.

Leading should be proportional to the point size used; one rule is to use leading 20% of the point size. However, to achieve certain visual effects, designers today use negative leading (when lines of text literally overlap one another). The amount depends on visual preference.

WIDOWS AND ORPHANS

People will argue over which is the orphan and which is the widow. For this book, a *widow* is the first line of a paragraph as the last line of the page (or column); an *orphan* is the last line of a paragraph, which is also the first line on the next page.

The important thing to remember is that they are both to be eliminated. You cannot avoid them, but you can correct them by adjusting the kerning and, if applicable, the line length. It takes time to manually fix all of the widows and orphans, but in the end, it gives you a professional looking design.

RIVERS

There are few things more distracting to typography then rivers in text. A river is the apparent white space produced when poor or random word spacing is used. Newspapers are notorious for having rivers running through their text.

Rivers happen when word spaces are greater than the white space between

> But the black kitten had been finished with earlier in the afternoon, and so, while Alice was sitting curled up in a corner of the great arm-chair, half talking to herself and half asleep, the kitten had been h a v i n g a grand game of romps with the ball of worsted Alice had been trying to wind up, and had been rolling it up and down till it had all come undone again; and

Figure 16-4. Example of Rivers.

the lines, usually caused by forced justification. It can be corrected through kerning and line length adjustment. Rivers are simple visual distractions that can be removed with a little time and patience.

HOW TO FORMAT TEXT

There are several elements within text formatting that tend to be used incorrectly. They fall into the category of grammatical issues as opposed to design issues. Following are several of these elements, and their correct use:

BRACKETS, PARENTHESES, AND BRACES

People tend to group all of these as one. However, they are three different typographical uses and have their own guidelines for when to use them.

- **Brackets** Used to set off inserted matter not written or said by the author of the text

  The tree was not actually a Maple [sic].

- **Parentheses** Used to set off words of explanation or comment

  Fine art lithography starts with a limestone (*lithos* in Greek).

- **Braces** Rarely used; they can be found in mathematical equations when several items are contained as a unit. They are also never (as a rule) to be used in tables

  $a+b\{x-y\}+=.$

ELLIPSES

Ellipses are used to indicate to the reader that the person typing the text has deliberately omitted one or more words. It consists of three leader dots with one space in between each of them. The key is to treat each period as if it were a word.

Incorrect: "Have you ever seen two... alike?"
Correct: "Have you ever seen two . . . alike?"

What happens if the text you are omitting falls at the end of a sentence, or at the beginning of a new sentence? When omitted matter falls at the end of the sentence: "Have you ever seen two . . . . One day she saw them." The fourth leader acts as the period, ending the sentence, and the three leader dots indicate the omitted matter.

Sometimes the omitted matter falls at the *beginning* of the sentence: "Have you ever seen two girls so alike? . . . she saw them." Remember that the beginning matter has been omitted so the first word that we see is not capitalized. The key point to remember for any of these elements is to be consistent within the document.

If a whole paragraph is being omitted the rule is to run leader dots for one full line no matter how long it may be.

HYPHENS AND DASHES

There are three types of dashes:

- **Hyphen** This is used for minus signs, when a word is broken between syllables onto separate lines, words to be spelled out in text, or in compound words. For example, mother-in-law or W-o-w.

- **En Dash** This is used in place of the word through or to, as in a series of numbers: January 12–17, 10 a.m.–2 p.m. It is also used to indicate a future event. For example, Born 1899, died –. To insert an en dash on a Mac, press option+hyphen. On a PC press ALT then type 0150.

- **Em Dash** This indicates a break in a sentence or a change in thought. It is also used to indicate missing material. For example, "Here is the list —." It is also used to indicate a quoted author. For example, — Unknown. To insert an em dash on a Mac press shift+option+hyphen. On a PC, press ALT, then type 0151.

There are many more exceptions and rules when it comes to dashes and other elements of text formatting. *The Chicago Manual of Style* is an excellent resource that lists every example and rule for specific situations. The rules listed here are general guidelines.

NUMBERS

There are three types of numbers: Roman numerals, aligning/modern numbers, and old-style numbers. All three have specific times when they should and should not be used.

1234567890   1234567890

Aligning Numbers   Old Style Numbers

Figure 16-5. Difference in Number Style.

Roman numerals are to be used as page numbers in the place of old style numbers or aligning numbers when the numbers fall in the front matter of a book. Front matter is anything that comes before the text of a book, such as a table of contents, list of illustrations, images, or charts.

Old-style numbers are found in the expert sets of a typeface and should be used when available. An expert set is a part of a typeface family, purchased separately, that contains the extra items like small caps, ligatures, old-style numbers, and swash letters, to name a few. Old-style numbers should always be used if they are part of text copy, except for tables and charts, and with any capital letters. If old style numbers are not available, proper typography allows reducing the point size of modern numbers a bit.

LIGATURES

A ligature is two or more letters that are joined as a single glyph. A glyph is any letter, number, or character. Ligatures should be used whenever possible.

Figure 16-6. Letters Compared. Non-ligatures are on the top, ligatures on the bottom.

FOOTNOTES AND REFERENCE MARKS

There are two styles of reference marks, numbers and symbols. Numbers are to be used as superiors and are unlimited in how many you can use. Symbols for footnotes, on the other hand, are limited to the following seven (in order) then repeated:

* Asterisk
† Dagger
‡ Double dagger
§ Section mark
|| Parallel rules
¶ Pilcrow

TIP: When using footnotes, remember to make sure the footnote is 2 pt. smaller than the text to create a visual break for the reader.

When repeated, these symbols appear in pairs as the following: **, ††, ‡‡, §§, || ||, ¶¶, and so on. If you need any more than this, you should use superior numbers. All the symbols can be found within Key Caps Utility on a Mac or the Character Map on a PC.

QUOTATION MARKS VS. PRIME MARKS

This distinction is often confused. Quotation marks are used to enclose a direct quotation; the punctuation is placed inside the quotation marks when it is part of the original quotation.

"Quotation Marks"	"Prime Marks"
"Quotation Marks"	"Prime Marks"
"Quotation Marks"	**"Prime Marks"**

Figure 16-7. Examples of Quotation Marks vs. Prime Marks

Quotation marks are also used to indicate position. Prime marks are used only for measurement to indicate feet and inches, or to indicate navigation.

TABLES AND CHARTS

In QuarkXPress and Adobe InDesign, you can make tables and charts using the "Tab" feature to define the insertion point for each tab. Tabs are used to align columns of text and numbers. Using spaces to manually create columns will lead to uneven spacing and make editing very difficult. The first tab you set becomes the default.

HOW TO AVOID TYPE DESIGN PROBLEMS

REVERSED OR OVERPRINTING TYPE

The *Rule of 30* says do not overprint type on anything darker than a 30% tint, and do not reverse out less than a 30% tint. *Overprinting* type means you are printing over an area that has already been printed; *reversed out* refers to white text or shapes on a dark background. Never reverse a serif below 10 pt. or a sans serif below 8 pt. Making the type bold helps. Do not reverse italic type. It creates chances for trapping problems.

Limit reversed type to small blocks of copy in order to slow the reader down. Visually, the reversed type creates a halo around each letter that causes eye fatigue. Also, avoid reversing type thin serifs like Garamond or Copperplate. If you must, make the point size of reversed type one or two points larger than non-reversed type.

COLORED TYPE

Here again, use the Rule of 30. Using opposite colors adds difficulty in reading. Light type on a dark background creates problems if the type has small serifs. It has to do with the trapping. You cannot print a light color on a dark color. A knockout has to be implemented, and knockouts for text with thin serifs leave a high chance for white halos due to misregistration.

CHAPTER 17

What You See Is Not Always What You Get

There are many reasons why color can alter when printed. One of the causes over which you, as the designer, have the most control, is called *color gamut*.

Remember the different boxes of crayons you had when you were a child? The box of twenty-four was enough for basic scribbles, but the box with one hundred twenty let your imagination run wild — with colors like tangerine, lilac, and "flesh" (peach). The final press your job is printed on is like the twenty-four crayon box. Go ahead and design with an extensive palette, but know that later someone will have to copy your colors within the limitations of the equivalent of the twenty-four crayon box; this is called *tone compression*. The next chapter includes a section on color correction and color balance, focusing on how to get printable images.

RUNNING THE GAMUT:
AN OVERVIEW OF COLOR SPACES

The different color spaces are like the different boxes of crayons. By looking at a gamut comparison, you can see the difference. A program called X-Rite ColorShop generated the gamut maps shown in Figure 17-1. A *gamut map* is when the colors that will print, or that will display on a monitor, are shown against the human visual spectrum. In ColorShop, you can load in your monitor profile and compare it to the profile of the printing device used.

If a color is in the RGB zone but outside the CMYK zone, it is called *out of gamut*. If you design with hot pink or neon colors, they will look great on screen but terrible in print because they are outside the gamut of the press.

Figure 17-1. RGB vs. SWOP. These are two basic defaults, a generic RGB (monitor space) and generic SWOP. Some yellows and light cyan colors are printable, but outside what you will see on your monitor. Vibrant greens and pinks, deep blues, and some reds will not print.

RGB VS. CMYK: UNDERSTANDING ADDITIVE AND SUBTRACTIVE COLOR SPACES

The concept of additive and subtractive color can take years to understand. In art classes, we learn that the primaries are red, yellow, and blue, but in physics class, the primaries are red, green, and blue. Then you get to printing and the primaries are defined as cyan, magenta, and yellow. Who is right? They all are, of course. *Primary colors* are just basic color building blocks and, in different color spaces, the building blocks are different. Yet in the end they all interrelate. *Secondary color* refers to what happens when you mix two primaries in equal proportions.

The space in computer monitors and televisions is called *RGB* (red, green, and blue). Computer monitors use light and filters to create the colors you see. Basically, anywhere you have light projecting through filters towards the viewer's eye uses an RGB color space. Light starts as white (like sunlight), then filters (such as prisms) break it up into the primary colors of RGB.

When the additive primaries are mixed, we see yellow, magenta, and cyan. Obviously, in coloring with light, there are things you can do that you can not do in print mediums. Therefore, the RGB gamut is considered larger than the CMY gamut (for the most part). Since you start with black (darkness), and add light in order to see color, RGB is considered an *additive* color space.

Colors in print are achieved through cyan, magenta, yellow, and black (CMYK) inks, dyes, or toners. With ink on paper you start with the white (or

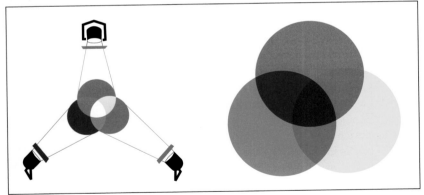

Figure 17-2.
Additive Color (left). In the theater, filters placed in front of spotlights create different colors on stage. Additive primaries are red, green, and blue. Mixing those gives you secondary colors of yellow, magenta, and cyan, and all three colors together make white.

Subtractive Color (right). Ink on paper uses cyan, magenta, and yellow primaries. When you look at the prism colors, you do not see magenta because for light-based color, mixing blue and red creates magenta, and those are at opposite ends in a rainbow, or prism.

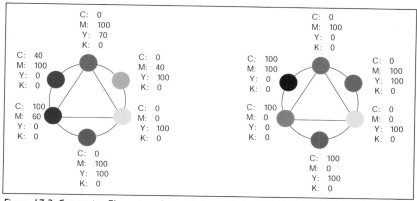

Figure 17-3. Comparing Elementary School Colors with Print Colors. The number values are from the CMYK sliders in Adobe Illustrator. In order to get the colors that children associate with the rainbow — red, orange, yellow, green, blue, violet (ROYGBV) — it is necessary to blend the CMYK values. On the right, you can see what happens with 100% values of the CMYK colorants. In order to approximate the version of red we are used to, printers have to mix a little less yellow into the ink. The same is true of the other colors. Only yellow and green remain fairly consistent.

base color) of the page; the more colors you pile on, the darker the color appears. The color is subtracted during the viewing process, thus the term *subtractive color*. In print, the color gamut is much smaller than that of a computer monitor. It makes sense that CMYK would appear less bright or colorful than RGB, since a proportion of light gets absorbed by the paper and the ink. A reproduction can never be as bright, detailed, or colorful as what you see in real life.

Why does this matter? If you are only dealing with RGB (i.e., design only for web, television, or movies), colors will not leap quite as far from one to the other. Going from RGB to CMYK is like fitting a square peg into a round hole; you have to design colors that can fit. If you do not, the colors shaved off will guarantee that the printed color will look wrong.

One thing that is not entirely true about the definitions of cyan, magenta, and yellow as primaries is that when you mix 100% of these, the color you see does not look like red, green, or blue. If you mix equal parts of cyan and magenta, you get a purplish color (printers use slightly different proportions to get a blue instead). If you mix equal amounts of magenta and yellow, you get an orange color, but using different proportions yields red. Cyan and yellow will create green. The inks used in a printing press inherently have little bits of the other colors blended in them, which make them impure. If it were possible to create pure inks, 100% cyan and 100% magenta would give you 200% blue. Instead, you have to use closer to 100% cyan and 90% magenta to get a blue color. The term printers use for this is *hue error*.

THE NUMBERS BEHIND COLOR CONVERSION: CIELAB

In 1931, the Commission International d'Eclairage (CIE) created a scientific color space. In 1976, this was refined and named CIE L*a*b*. The CIE attempted to define all color visible to an ideal human viewer in terms of three axes.

The vertical axis contains *lightness*, or luminance, or L* (L star). One end of the L* axis is white, the other end is black, with a range from 1–100. The second axis was the a* (a-star), which encompasses green (–128) at one end and red (+127) at the other. The total values between red and green are 255, which is the maximum number of gray values in an 8-bit system. Red and green are opposites on the hue wheel in the LAB model. The b* (b-star) axis is blue and yellow, also opposites on the hue wheel, at –128 (blue) and +127 (yellow). In between those three values (L, a*, and b*) are, theoretically, all the values of color visible to the human eye. On the gamut map shown earlier, the bigger horseshoe shape reflects the LAB color gamut.

When a color is converted from RGB to CMYK, the RGB values, (for example, a bright red with a value of red 203, blue 17, and green 37) are converted into LAB numbers. The RGB values translate into equivalent LAB numbers: luminance is 51 (scale of 1–100), a* is 62 (+127 is the reddest value possible), and b* is 54 (on the yellow side of the axis). Then from the LAB values, CMYK numbers are assigned. In this case, the numbers are 0% cyan, 86% magenta, 97% yellow, and 3% black.

In Figure 17-4, color sampler #1 is set on a red value in the picture. The info palette reflects what is occurring at that spot. The RGB values show that the color is predominantly in the red channel. The LAB values show that the color is fairly luminous, and positively on the red and yellow side of the hue axes; in CMYK it is clear that the color is a blend of mostly magenta and yellow ink with a tiny touch of black.

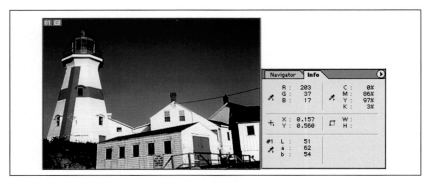

Figure 17-4. The LAB Values Behind an RGB to CMYK Conversion.

The LAB gamut is bigger than any printable gamut, and bigger than any RGB gamut out there. Why not use it for everything? Since the gamut is so much larger, every printing device and every monitor would alter an image in LAB mode because it would undergo constant color compression. While it may not work well for a permanent image mode, it is great to use for color correction and sharpening.

COLOR PROBLEMS

SPOT COLOR VS. PROCESS COLOR

The convenience of swatch palettes, and not understanding what they entail on the press, can complicate the color aspect of the job. All the swatch palettes, in Macromedia FreeHand, Adobe Illustrator, QuarkXPress, and so on generate spot colors (for a more thorough discussion of spot color, refer to Chapter 7). A spot color is a premixed ink that is put into a separate printing unit. That means that any job with a spot color would have to run through a four-color press twice. If you leave those colors in the palettes of your drawing, imaging, and layout files, and neither you nor the printer convert to process, your job will generate films or plates for however many spot colors you included in the design. When you want spot colors, they are a wonderful thing, but when you do not, they are very expensive. This is another reason why a printer will return your design for you to correct before they will go to print.

HI-FI AND HEXACHROME COLOR

Hi-Fi color is actually a color solution since it begins to extend the printable gamut. Pantone added a vivid orange and vibrant green to the base CMYK colors, and called it Hexachrome. Pantone claims that with those extra colors, they can replicate most of their spot colors. This extends the printable color gamut, making it possible to print neon colors and other brighter shades than are not possible with CMYK process colors alone. With an extended gamut, many of the colors visible on the monitor are available for printing.

DESIGNER EXPECTATIONS

Your computer screen is not reliable. The next chapter covers some solutions you can use to get the color on your monitor to more closely match the print. There are RGB modes on your computer that try to keep things within a printable gamut, Adobe 1998 and ColorMatch RGB. Unless you are designing for video, try to avoid using things like wide-gamut RGB.

What you see on your monitor sets up expectations as you design. If you do not want to be disappointed in the printed result, it is better to use a monitor setting that more closely reflects what is possible in print.

EDUCATING YOUR CLIENTS

When you are selling an idea to a client, you will usually print it on the best paper and best printer available. That is great for making the sale, but what happens when the final version comes back and the colors are less vibrant than in the proof? It is not the printer's fault. The problem is that proofing devices often have a larger gamut than printing presses.

If you have to use such a proofing device, be sure to inform your client that it may look different from the press. But you are better off showing a print within the range of an average printing press. Another element of meaningful proofs is using the same paper that will be used on press. If your proof is on coated paper but you are printing on uncoated, the color will look different. Many paper suppliers will be happy to give you a free sample of paper to use for proofing, and printers may also give you some samples of paper if you ask.

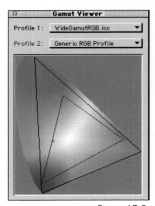

Figure 17-5.
Wide Gamut vs. Generic RGB.
Wide-gamut is an option in your computer for the colors on your monitor. It comes close to most of the colors the human eye can see. That is an exciting possibility if you never leave RGB mode.

Many if not all color problems can be dealt with if you adjust your expectations. A phrase that printers use is, "Every job is a custom job." Even though there are always forces beyond your control, if you take care of your end, at least you will not be the one paying to redo the job.

CHAPTER 18

MAKING COLOR WORK

Historically, prepress professionals managed color. Today's computer-driven world requires that designers understand the process of color management if they want to ensure consistent color.

For colors to remain consistent, you have to trust the numbers and not the screen. If your system is properly calibrated then (in theory) your monitor can be used for *soft proofing* (proofing the screen image). It is as if each device in the design chain has numbers that talk to each other, and you have to facilitate the conversation. You should have an understanding of the languages at work and learn to negotiate the translations. If you follow some basic principles, color chaos can be minimized.

The two big areas involved in achieving consistent color are correcting and balancing image colors, and color managing your workflow.

FOUR-COLOR TRANSITIONS

In getting color to print, four areas of transition are involved: getting the image into the computer, manipulating the image inside the computer, creating meaningful proofs, and sending the job to a commercial printer. Each area contains its own color space, its own set-up needs, and its own limitations. Getting from one area to the next involves a transition of data, and that transition is usually where color is affected.

1. The image is usually imported into the computer via scanner or digital camera; this is the RGB stage.

2. The second stage is getting the color you want on screen and in proofs, which involves a calibrated monitor, tone compression, proper neutrals, correct memory colors, image sharpening, and any necessary color correction. While viewed on screen, this stage can be referred to as the soft-proofing stage. Images are usually still in RGB, though they can be converted to CMYK.

3. The third transition is making proofs for your own evaluation, for the client, and for the commercial printer. This can only be done in CMYK.

4. Finally, of course, is the transition from your color space to that of the commercial printer, who will output the final high-end version. While this seems intimidating at first, once understood, it provides the key to being in control of the mysterious world of color.

COLOR BALANCE AND COLOR CORRECTION

Once an image is in the computer, there are basic steps to achieving consistent color:

1. Set your goals.

2. Set up your color spaces and profiles.

3. Set your dot gain (tone reproduction).

4. Set your highlights and shadows (tone compression).

5. Use the right tools (selective color).

6. Convert at the right time (RGB to CMYK) with the right intent.

7. Sharpen the image.

8. Correct the color based on a proof, not the screen.

When using these steps, you will usually be correcting an image based on numbers in Photoshop's Info palette. However, to achieve consistent color from printer to printer, you might want to invest the time, money, and energy to learning about color management.

SET YOUR GOALS

Before trying to correct the color in an image, it is helpful to know what your goal is. Where will the image be used? If it will be used on the Internet, the CMYK issues are no concern; if going to other venues, you want to ensure the color remains consistent by using the smallest gamut in the array of potential outputs.

SETTING THE RECOMMENDED RGB (SCREEN) SPACE

As was mentioned previously, a computer monitor uses an RGB color gamut. The color tone, brightness, contrast, and range are dependent on controls that you set. If you have installed an Adobe program, then Adobe Gamma was automatically installed. This has a screen that will walk you through setting up your computer monitor so that the color space is consistent.

Assuming your monitor is calibrated properly, you also need to select the RGB settings that are compatible with a print-oriented workflow.

Gamma is a curve that controls the brightness of the midtones, *white point* is based on the warmth or coolness of light, and *primaries* are the photons (or LCDs) that control how your monitor uses light to render color on screen.

SETTING A CMYK (PRINT) SPACE

There are many different CMYK options. As discussed, you need cyan, magenta, yellow, and black colorants in order to print. However, different presses use ink or toner sets that render colors differently. For example, the magazine industry uses a cooler magenta than newspaper production (i.e., SWOP vs. SNAP inks). The best option is to find out from your printer what settings they would like you to use; many will have profiles available online. The definitions discussed in this section will help you communicate clearly with your printer about what to select.

SELECTING A CUSTOM CMYK SPACE

If a printer gave you CMYK profile values to use, your software will have a CMYK customization option where you will generate appropriate printing values. Here are the key elements in printing a job.

- **Name** If you do choose to customize a CMYK setting, be sure to name your file consistently. It is a good idea to include the press, paper, ink colors, dot gain, and GCR amount; for example, "Speedmaster (Coated) SWOP, 23%, Medium."

- **Ink Colors** This indicates the colorant set that will be used. You can place a service provider's ink set in your ColorSync folder, then access it here. SWOP is the default option. The publishers of *Time* and other magazines came together on an ink set that worked well in their printing conditions and standardized the values. It consists of the other values found on the screen.

- **Dot Gain** The average dot gain for web offset printing on coated paper will be 20%. Dot gain builds in a compensation curve so that data sent to the imagesetter will be 20% smaller than the final print output. Once the dots gain on press, the result is the desired one.

- **Separation Type** UCR (*undercolor removal*) and GCR (*gray component replacement*) are two different methods printers use to retain image quality while using less ink. In slight, but significantly different ways, they find neutral values of cyan, magenta, and yellow inks and replace them with corresponding black values. When in doubt, leave the option at Gray Component Replacement and set the Black Generation amount to medium (the defaults in Photoshop).

- **Black Generation** As stated, it is best — unless a prepress operator tells you otherwise — to use medium. *Black generation* sets the amount of black replacement used during gray component replacement. A maximum setting means that black will be substituted for every neutral pixel.

- **Black Ink Limit** The SWOP default is 95%, which means that a black dot of 95% is the last dot the press can hold without *plugging up* (when dot gain and ink thickness combine to completely fill the line screen sooner than they should).

- **Total Ink Limit** In process printing, there are four colors; the theoretical maximum total ink is 400%. For most press conditions, that number will oversaturate the paper and lead to the paper getting wet and therefore wavy. SWOP default is 300%.

- **UCA (Undercolor Addition)** After taking out color with GCR, you can then add it back in with UCA. This is mostly used in newsprint applications; just leave it at 0% unless someone in the prepress department tells you otherwise.

SETTING GRAY VALUES (TONE REPRODUCTION)

In order for your image to print correctly, it is necessary to compensate for dot gain. This is a very simple procedure. Use a standard guide like GRACoL or SNAP, and follow their directions for the kind of paper you will be using. GRACoL includes a Printing Guidelines section that contains a chart of input variables, which include the paper or substrate, line screen, *total area coverage* (TAC, the same thing as black ink limit in Photoshop), and the solid ink density (the thickness of that layer of ink, as read by a densitometer).

Then there are output print characteristics, including *total dot gain %*, which is the dot gain for that color in the 50% dot. In order to compensate, you have to adjust the curves for your ink set in Adobe Photoshop.

SETTING HIGHLIGHTS AND SHADOWS (TONE COMPRESSION)

A reality faced by color photographers is that their images will never look as vibrant in print as on film. Photographers scan in slides or negatives, and the color on screen still looks great, but when converted to a printable gamut, the colors can seem dull. This is the reality of the smaller CMYK gamut. The process of squeezing the larger film gamut into a printable range is called *tone compression*. Once an image is scanned, printable highlight and shadow points must be selected.

> **TIP:** To make sure there are good highlight and shadow details to use, you can scan the image with a grayscale.

If not, you risk printing an image where someone's forehead shows up as a pure white, or the shadows in the image become a solid black mass. A highlight is not 100% white and a shadow is not 100% black — those values give you unprintable highlights and shadows. There needs to be just enough color information in the highlight area to create tiny dots in the halftones, and just enough shadow so that the dots do not all join together into a tar pit.

Figure 18-1. Before selecting a highlight and shadow point (left), the light areas of the boys face, arm, and the right of the background are too light to print and would look "blown out" in print. After selecting highlight and shadow values (right), the image is in a printable gamut. The boy's arm and man's shirt will have detail.

A *highlight* is the brightest neutral white in an image that is not a reflection or a light source (light on water, or the sun itself); a *shadow* is the darkest point in the image. By following these guidelines, you will correct most color casts and instantly have better looking prints.

USE THE RIGHT TOOLS: PHOTOSHOP COLOR CORRECTION

Now that you have compressed the tones in your image, you are ready to ensure the right color values. While using the highlight and shadow selection will eradicate much of an image's color cast, you may need, for example, to clear up a tiny yellowish shade in your highlights. Adobe Photoshop has many powerful tools that allow you to affect the color of your image. Some tools give you more control than others. The tools that create radical change without letting you control how much should be avoided.

There are three kinds of color correction: *reproduction correction*, where you change the image to ensure printable values; *memory*

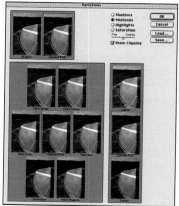

Figure 18-2. The Variations Tool. The amount of change ranges from fine to coarse; compare your original image with your proposed alteration.

Good Tools	Tools to Use with Caution
Curves This tool is for the advanced user. It permits a very fine degree of control. Use of an adjustment layer (Photoshop 5 and 6) means that you do not alter the pixel data until you flatten the image.	
Levels This tool allows you to pick highlights and shadows and alter the midtones of the image by moving the slider back and forth. It offers control without having to think quite as much as the curves tool requires.	**Brightness/Contrast** Creates an overall BIG change that causes information data to be permanently lost.
Gaussian Blur The only blur tool that lets you control the amount of blur. It works very well in LAB mode as one of the steps in correcting for visual noise.	*Any of the other blur tools* None of the other blur tools let you control the amount. You might want to play with them for special effects, but they are not as good for regular image correction.
Unsharp Mask You are in charge of the degree and kind of sharpening to use.	*Sharpening Filter* The program decides how much to sharpen the image.
REPLACE COLOR This tool allows you to click with the eyedropper on a color in your image to change it. It will change every pixel with the same color data, so you will affect both a red dress and a red apple in the same scene. Use this tool with an image mask in order to limit what is affected. This is great for editorial color changes.	DESATURATE Found under Image>Adjust>Desaturate, this creates grayscale values. This can be used for special effects, like creating duotone effects without a mode change. However, it is a radical change without any way to control how the change is done.
Color Balance An acceptable backup for selective color, but not a first choice.	**Hue/Saturation** Use this as the last resort. It is acceptable, but not as controlled as selective color.

Figure 18-16. Tools in **Bold** *can be created as adjustment layers through either Image>Adjust Layer> New Adjustment Layer, or in Photoshop 6.0 and higher by clicking on the black and white circle at the bottom of the Layers palette.*

Items in Italic are Filters.

Items in SMALL CAPS *are under Image>Adjust.*

Good Tools	Tools to Use with Caution
Selective Color	DUST AND SCRATCHES
This is the primary tool to use for color correction. When you set it to relative, you will create subtle changes. It is okay most of the time to leave it on absolute. You can change colors in your whites, your grays, your midtones, and in other color channels. To use this tool effectively, you need a good grasp on the relationship between additive and subtractive color.	This blurs the image pixels in an attempt to disguise any dust or scratches in the scan. Your image gets softened enough during reproduction, so there is no reason for this.
	ANY AUTO BUTTONS
	It is better to know what is happening to your file. Anything automatic should be suspect until you know what it is doing.

color correction, usually in objects that "should be" a certain color, such as red apples or blue sky; and *editorial correction*, where you change the image to please the client.

The variations tool, found under Image>Adjust>Variations, is intuitive and easy to use. Variations serves as training wheels to eventually using *selective color*. It gives you an on-screen preview with a color wheel set-up. Using Variations will help you to understand which colors are opposite in the additive/subtractive color world. The problem is that correction is based on your monitor. If you combine that with proper use of the Info palette, it can be a relatively direct color correction tool. Variations do not provide the precision of a professional level of working. As you learn more, you will outgrow the variations tool, but it is a good start.

Remember the guiding principle in prepress design is working with the end in mind. If possible, it is better to print a proof before starting to adjust the color too much. Often the correct CMYK setting, tone reproduction, and tone compression will take care of getting the color in gamut.

SOFT-PROOFING ON A MONITOR

If your monitor is not calibrated, you cannot use it to judge color. It can give you a rough idea, but *do not rely* on an uncalibrated monitor. Use the Info palette to evaluate the true color, not just what it looks like.

In theory, ColorMatch RGB or Adobe RGB will build in a level of soft proofing, but if the image is not converted to the working space, this will not happen. The idea with soft proofing is that the monitor should reflect your printer's output, so that when you make changes to the image on the screen, it matches the way the image will look in print. While this is not always a perfect match, it certainly gets you in the ballpark. If you leave the monitor set-up at wide-gamut RGB, what you see on screen is *not* what you get. Your Adobe software provides a custom-proofing option that will reflect you end-use needs.

UNDERSTANDING RGB-TO-CMYK CONVERSION

Before creating your final version, call your service provider and ask them if they want you to convert your images to CMYK, or if they would rather do it. Any conversion can lead to loss of some of the color data in the file, and once you save the converted image, that data is gone forever. If you convert it to the wrong CMYK space, the prepress department may have to convert it back to RGB and then create a new CMYK version — two unnecessary conversions. If they ask you to convert the file, ask them for a profile, or at least what settings they want you to use in the Custom CMYK screen. Remember to retain both an RGB and a CMYK version of the file so that you can repurpose the RGB file for various printers and multimedia purposes.

When you do convert your image, depending on your goal for the image, there are different conversion intents possible. If you select Advanced Mode in the Color Settings screen, you will see a Conversion Option screen at the bottom of the Color Settings screen.

The "intent" is an option you will find in many different programs, and it deserves a closer look. You will also find these rendering intents when you convert to profile. There are four options under the Intent tab: perceptual, saturation, relative colorimetric, and absolute colorimetric. These options relate to what side you want the computer to err on. As a color conversion is happening, there may be colors outside of one gamut or the other. This is your chance to instruct the computer how to handle such sticky situations.

- **Perceptual** To keep the range of colors in an image so that all the colors still look natural even if the actual numeric values switch.

- **Saturation** Each color as intense as possible.

- **Relative Colorimetric** Used for graphics like logos. It means that the computer should factor in the white of the page, and then try to keep the numeric values of the color identical. This works fine if all your source colors are inside the gamut of the destination profile. If any colors are outside, they get clipped; a pink tone outside the CMYK gamut might end up looking the same as an orange value that was inside the CMYK gamut.

- **Absolute Colorimetric** Does not factor in the white point of the paper, so the numbers have to match exactly or they get clipped. This leads to a more precise color match (important for logos and other devices that require consistent color), but risks even more clipping than does relative colorimetric.

Before converting anything from RGB to CMYK, make sure the settings are correct: your RGB and CMYK are custom set. Now the question is, when should you convert? There are debates over this issue; here is one efficient option. You want to control CMYK settings, so create a copy of the RGB file and convert the copy to CMYK. Make sure to label each file appropriately: "name.rgb.tif" and "name.cmyk.tif." Use the copy in your layout program. If you know the output values, use those in CMYK setup. It is a good idea to retain the saved RGB version. Many prepress providers would rather have color conversion under their control.

A COLOR MANAGEMENT PRIMER

ENSURING THE RIGHT COLOR: CALIBRATING AND PROFILING

It is a relatively simple concept; *calibration* simply makes sure a piece of equipment operates in a consistent manner. Over time, monitors, printers, and scanners shift in how they render color. Calibration herds drifting values back to where they should be. Without this, for example, you may have a yellowish cast to your monitor. If you alter image quality based on the screen, you will be surprised by the color when it prints. During calibration, the yellow is adjusted to ensure a neutral gray.

Profiling measures what a calibrated device is producing, calculates the difference between those measurements and the ideal values, and produces a descriptive file to compensate for the differences. This file allows your system to compensate in order to produce the ideal values. Profiling has a few basic elements:

- A calibrated device: monitor, printer, scanner, commercial printing press, etc.

- A *known target*: values of a target have been measured and distributed.

- A version of the target rendered by the calibrated device: scanned version of the target, for example.

- A *profile editor* program: takes the ideal, known values and compares them with the values produced by the calibrated device, measures the differences, and produces a profile.

If a print device tends to print pinkish gray instead of neutral gray, even after calibration, a profile will tell the computer to put a bit less magenta in the mix when the file is processed, and the printed dots will print neutral gray. While the process is simple, it can be time consuming and the equipment can be expensive.

Creating a profile for your desktop scanner and printer will yield proofs with consistent color. Using profiles from a pre-press service or a commercial printer lets you make sure that what you view on your monitor and proof on your printer will more closely reflect what will happen on press than the system you have now. This is the primary solution to making sure that what you see on screen will be what you get in print.

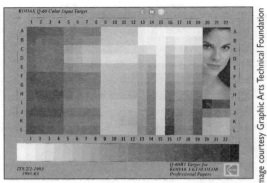

Figure 18-3. An IT-8 Target, Used to Profile Scanners. One of the first places you will notice a color cast is skin tone; people have a strong sense of how it "should" look. The photo allows for a quick visual evaluation of how a scanner or printer handles color.

CALIBRATION AND PROFILING OF VARIOUS DEVICES

There are many image sources: digital cameras, scanners, photo CDs, the Web, and so on. The data you place in your computer is called input. Consistent color output requires predictable input. A photo CD should have a source profile available. Web images will rarely have embedded profiles. Since you have no idea what the source profile was, use a generic RGB profile like ColorMatch RGB.

- Contact the equipment manufacturer and ask if they have calibration targets available.

- You can also have a professional from a service bureau calibrate and profile all of your equipment. The advantage is you do not have to deal with all this; the disadvantage is that calibration should be done daily, and profiling needs to be done every month.

CALIBRATING A SCANNER

Most scanners have some level of self-calibration; the more expensive the scanner, the more reliable the calibration. Figure 18-4 shows the self-calibrating strips on a drum scanner. Every time the drum begins a scan, it self-calibrates from the transparent and white strips. Check if your scanner lets you access that white strip, and keep it clean.

On a scanner, calibration involves scanning a target, then making sure that white area values add up to a neutral white, for one example. If they do not, the scanner needs to be adjusted so that it is not introducing any color casts,

Figure 18-4. Scanner Self-Calibration on a Howtek Desktop Drum Scanner. The white and clear bands are there to establish the lightest point for either reflective or transparent image.

or lightening or darkening an image. A color cast is when a scanner, camera, or printer makes an image appear to have an overall color hue. For example, old color photos from the 1960s often have an overall orange color cast.

Scanners perform a self-calibration from an embedded white strip before each scan they make. The reality though is that those white strips can get dusty, or have the color shift over time. As a result, a scanner should ideally be calibrated before each scanning session, and should be profiled once a month. Fortunately, once you have the gear, calibrating and profiling a scanner is quick and easy.

PROFILING A SCANNER

Once a scanner is calibrated, profiling is easy. You need a target and a profile-editing program. All you have to do is scan the target, let the profile editor compare the input values with the target data (often accessible online), name the profile so that you can find it again, and save it in your ColorSync (Mac OS) or ICM (Windows) folder. Use the saved profile as the source profile for anything scanned on that device.

A source profile means the profile from the device that created the file. If you get the image from a photo CD, then the CD manufacturer should have a source profile. If you create the image on screen, then your monitor profile would be the source profile. A *destination* profile is a profile of the printing device that the file is going to.

NOTE: Digital camera profiles work only if you have a constant lighting system in place. Follow directions from the camera manufacturer for calibrating the camera. For profiling, take the raw camera file and convert it to an appropriate RGB space.

Quite often, this will be a SWOP profile. Because SWOP was created for the magazine industry, it will not have values that exactly correspond to the press you may be using, but most commercial printers are able to match their press to SWOP specifications. In cases where you do not have a known destination, but have to create a CMYK file, use SWOP as the "generic" CMYK profile.

CALIBRATING A MONITOR

There are two ways to calibrate a monitor. The first is inexpensive and is subjective; the second is expensive, but objective. Most computer monitors arrive with a default monitor setting at 9300K, a cool blue color. *Color temperature* is measured in degrees Kelvin; higher numbers are cooler bluish colors, and lower numbers are warm, yellowish colors. Monitor calibration is designed to achieve the neutral gray color temperature, which is ideal. It is best to calibrate your monitor every 2–4 weeks. The inexpensive, less than ideal option is Adobe Gamma, which is placed automatically in your system folder when you install an Adobe product. The more expensive, but objective option is an external calibration device.

WARNING: Hardly any of this monitor calibration applies to the LCD monitors found on most laptops and in flat-screen desktop monitors. If you have a desktop LCD monitor, there are external devices available that hang in front of the monitor to calibrate. If you change the angle you sit from the monitor, you affect your color perception of items on screen.

The Subjective Method: Adobe Gamma A subjective calibration is not ideal because through the day, your eyes grow tired and affect how you see color. The lighting in the room, sunlight from the windows, the reflection of a t-shirt, can all affect how you perceive color on screen. The following terms will help you become familiar with the elements of monitor calibration:

- *Brightness and contrast* are adjustable internally, or externally on the knobs on your monitor. Do not adjust the knobs. After you calibrate your monitor, take care not to touch the knobs. Changing the amount of light coming through the screen will drastically affect the appearance of your colors.

- *Phosphors* vary with the type of monitor. Your owner's manual should state which kind you own; select that kind here. Big, boxy monitors are *cathode-ray tube* monitors and have light that shines through filters; those monitors contain phosphors that deteriorate over time. Newer, flat *liquid-crystal display* (LCD) monitors do not contain phosphors at all; rather florescent light projects through liquid crystals and color filters. The advantage is that there are no phosphors to decay; the drawback is that if the angle of the screen changes so does the color quality. That makes it difficult to calibrate an LCD; as you slouch, you affect the visible quality of the color.

- *Gamma* adjusts the lightness and darkness of the display. Gamma means the lightness factor of the midtones of an image. Even if you are on a PC, you might want to try Mac gamma of 1.8, as it is lighter and brighter than PC gamma of 2.2. This is one of the reasons Web designers tell you that PC images will display darker than Mac images — the gamma default is darker on a PC than on a Mac.

- *White point* defaults at 9300K, a cool blue. Use 5000K for graphic arts standards, though this can appear a bit yellow as a monitor color. Photography uses 6500K, a cool neutral, as the standard. The industry is still in flux about which is better for use on computer monitors. The lower the number, the warmer the light tone emitted.

The Objective Method: An External Device If you are serious about color management, you need to purchase a hardware device to calibrate your monitor (again, this applies to CRT monitors).

There are many monitor calibration devices available. They either attach onto your monitor, or hang in front of it. This device measures different color points and then adjusts them to target settings. The process is automatic and takes around ten minutes. The advantage is that this is an automatic, objective calibration. A hardware device does not have the subjective handicaps of the human eye, which perceives color differently depending on the time of day, surrounding colors, and lighting conditions. Once the monitor is calibrated, you are prompted to name the profile; pick something that includes the date and a name you will remember.

> **WARNING:** Do not use a calibration device that attaches to a monitor with an LCD monitor. The suction cups will damage. Instead, order a hanging calibration device that hovers in front of the screen.

GENERATING PRINTER PROFILES

Generating a printer profile involves printing a target from a digital source (like the Kodak web site) or from a scanned target. Usually the target is the IT-8. The printed color blocks have to be measured by a spectrophotometer or a densitometer. Both are hardware devices that measure how thick the layer of ink is and what the color appears to be.

Depending on the number of color blocks in the target, manual measurement can take hours. There are machines to do this automatically. Of course, all this gets quite expensive. If you get serious about color management, you will need to work closely with your printer manufacturer and your service providers to establish a workflow that will make sense for your own needs.

> **TIP:** When you are going to a specific commercial press, call ahead and find out if they have a profile available. Use the commercial press profile as the CMYK profile when converting from RGB to CMYK. If they do not have a profile available, try the SWOP default; but check with your service provider first.

USING ICC PROFILES

The *International Color Consortium* (ICC) was a group of companies that created color standardization practices for the graphic arts. The good news is that all the profiles of your scanner, printer, etc. are considered ICC profiles.

THINGS TO REMEMBER ABOUT MAKING COLOR WORK

- If you own an expensive scanner, consider investing in profiling equipment.

- A less expensive scanner is good for Web images, but not for print quality scans. Use the calibration tools that come with it, and pay for better quality scans if you want to print on a lithographic press.

- Set up your monitor so the color reflects print conditions; then make sure not to touch those knob adjustments.

- Set up your RGB and CMYK working spaces and stay in RGB until the last possible moment.

- Check the gamut warning on your RGB files and adjust them until they fit into a printable gamut. Otherwise, the color may go haywire.

- Communicate with your service bureau and/or commercial printer so that you create realistic proofs, and therefore realistic expectations, for yourself and for your clients.

- Evaluate color based on the numbers in the Info palette, and not based on what you see on your monitor.

CHAPTER 19

PROOFING

A *proof* is a printed test sheet that is examined to check for flaws and errors. It also acts as a prediction of the results you will get off the press. Knowing if the print is right before it goes to press can save costly time on the press and wasted money for inks and papers. Proofing quality varies from machine to machine. It is important to know what kind of quality a proofing machine is capable of when evaluating a proof.

A proof must be viewed under constant, controlled conditions. A neutral surrounding and viewing booth is best, because outside factors such as different lighting conditions can affect the appearance of color. The way to evaluate a proofer's quality is to look at three components: the *colorants*, the substrate printed on, and how the proofing device simulates tone reproduction.

CHOOSING WHICH PROOFING METHOD TO USE

Print jobs go through three proofing stages; different types of proofs are referred to by more than one name. It is important to carefully check the proofs at all three stages because they pinpoint where the mistakes are occurring, who is responsible for them, and who should pay for corrections.

DESKTOP PROOFS

Desktop proofs are also called preliminary proofs, or pre-proofing. There are two types of preliminary proofs: the *soft proof* and the *hard proof*. You probably use preliminary proofing without even knowing it. Any time you look at your project on a monitor or a print to evaluate it, you are proofing.

The *soft proof* is what you see on a monitor. It is cheap, quick, and uses no chemicals or consumables. It is very important to keep in mind that what is appearing on a computer monitor will not appear the same as a printed product. It is used for checking initial positioning. It is also used for *relative* color checking. That means seeing if it is green or red. Soft proofing should not be used for any sort of exact color checking. Soft proofing depends on the calibration of color monitors. As desktop systems improve, such adjustments will become more automatic. But no matter how well calibrated your monitor may be, any critical color judgments should be made from a hard copy proof.

Color displays generate color by illuminating combinations of phosphors in the common additive primaries (red, green, and blue,) and varying the intensity of the electron beams exciting the phosphor. Print works in the subtractive primaries CMYK. Therefore, something in RGB is not capable of appearing the same in CMYK.

Hard proofs are the printouts you make on your desktop printer. These are also not used to evaluate color accurately. They do not use the same substrates, colorants, or tone reproduction as the press the final product will be printed on. Desktop proofs have very poor quality capabilities. Remember that your desktop printer needs to be consistent in its output in order for you to get the most out of the proofs it creates. Color should only be considered accurate if your system is color managed. If not, the dyes in desktop printers may not match the colors that will be output to films for separations.

Desktop printers are not halftone or PostScript printers, and therefore cannot accurately represent tone reproduction of the press. This is the cheapest and simplest proofing system. It can be a black-and-white or color inkjet or laser printer. It catches the mistakes that are so easily avoided and can save time and money. If your design will not print correctly to your desktop printer, do not expect it to print on a more expensive service bureau printer.

What Do Desktop Proofs Check For?

- **Text placement** Is text where is should be, using the correct typeface?
- **Image placement** Are the images present and where they should be?
- **Image cropping, size, and positioning** Do the images look right?
- **Typos** Is your entire text proofed?
- **Overall appearance** Is it what you expected?

OFF-PRESS PROOFS

These are proofs, either analog or digital, created by the prepress department or a service bureau. Typically, these are used for *contract proofs*, which is a proof given to a client to sign off on as a form of a contract implying that they agree with what they see on the proof and it is ready to go to press.

Analog proofs are made from output film separations. Using one of the many proofing systems (like Imation MatchPrint), a piece of paper coated with a special UV laminate is exposed to each individual film separation and a color toner for each film separation. Analog proofs are also known as photopolymer laminate systems. The sheets of color toner are usually made up of the same pigments used on press, but that is not always the case. Make sure to ask if you are using that proof to determine color quality; this will provide the same colors and hue error that will be found on press. For example, if the press uses SWOP-coated standards, the proofing materials the prepress department will use are SWOP-coated materials.

The substrate onto which the color is laminated comes in two options, premade papers and the actual paper that the final project will be printed on. Premade papers are made by the proofing manufacturers and come in several grades such as commercial and newsprint. This is not recommended because it is not a completely accurate representation of the final print, depending on the actual substrate being run through the press. The other option is to use the actual paper the final project will be printed on, which is much more accurate and will give you a good idea of what the colors will look like on the substrate to be used.

Bluelines made from films are a form of analog proofing that are still used by many people. The films are exposed to a light-sensitive paper. Bluelines are good for mock-ups because they can be folded and bound easily. However, they cannot show process color; they only show the interaction between color breaks, which makes them good for two- and three-color jobs. If a proof for a four-color or more job is needed, a different proofing process is advisable.

Digital proofs are proofs made directly from an electronic file, using machines that are calibrated to meet industry standards for color matching and are capable of high resolution. The ones capable of resolutions 1800 dpi or higher can actually produce halftone dots.

Some clients are uncomfortable with digital proofs. It is hard to change over from the analog proofs that they have come to rely on for years. Another reason for hesitation on the client's part is because some digital proofs produce continuous-tone images rather than halftone dots. Digital proofs are capable of high turnaround times due to the use of a digital file, computer RIP speeds, and machine flexibility, allowing for a close, if not accurate, color match for almost any printing condition.

There are many different proofing machines on the market that meet a variety of needs, from CMYK, to Hexachrome, to spot and metallic capabilities. As technology continues to evolve, new changes are made everyday to improve proofing quality. As of today however, there are several different categories with distinct advantages and disadvantages.

What Do Off-Press Proofs Check For?

- Color quality and registration.
- Imposition.
- Trim, crop, and fold marks, if applicable.
- Density and tonal reproduction.
- Dot gain and moiré problems.

DIGITAL PROOFERS

This section describes some of the current categories of digital proofers on the market. The important point to remember is that there are three key factors to know when evaluating a proof: the colorant used, the substrate printed on, and the method used to simulate halftones. These three factors will tell you right away, even before you see the proof, how well the proof will indicate the final printed product. The closer these factors are to the final printing process used, the better prediction you will have. Ask the printer or service provider what their equipment uses and how it compares to the final printing process.

CAUTION: It is important to remember that an off-press proof is *not an exact representation* of what the final printed product will look like. Factors such as substrate, inks, press, and many others can affect the appearance of the final product.

DYE DIFFUSION

The first category of digital proofing machines are *dye-diffusion* proofers. This technology is probably the furthest from what will be seen on press, since it uses dyes that are different from the pigments used on press. Therefore, the printers will have to work harder to match the press pigments; the colors will just not look the same. Dye-diffusion proofing machines are not capable of printing on the actual press paper; they require their own polyester papers, which come in various brightness levels to simulate different press substrates. However, it will obviously not appear the same because different papers interact with ink in different ways. Finally, the dye-diffusion proofing machines are not halftone systems. The RIP controls the transfers of colorant. Because of these factors, dye diffusion should not be used for contract proofs.

PIGMENT DIFFUSION

The next category is *pigment diffusion*. As its name indicates, this technology uses pigments — the same pigments that are used on press — which make colors more accurate. The substrates used are polyester, which is then laminated onto any paper. However, it is found through testing that it is actually limited to *coated* stock. Just as in the dye-diffusion proofing machines, dot gain is controlled by the RIP and can be calibrated to different settings.

INKJET PRINTERS

These are continuous-tone printers, which use dots to make up images and text. They differ from desktop inkjet printers because they have a separate RIP, which controls dot gain. The RIP is vital for prepress inkjet proofs. The inks in these printers are actually dye colorants (some inkjet printers are capable of using pigments). The substrates vary. Inkjet proofers are very popular in the newspaper industry because they can print on the actual uncoated newsprint. They can not, however, print on actual coated press paper. Coatings do not allow the inks to absorb into the paper fibers, so the ink will never dry. Special papers with different brightness levels are made by the manufacturer to try to closely simulate press conditions.

THERMAL TRANSFER

Thermal transfer technology is the next category of proofing systems available. Thermal transfer technology is capable of printing at 2400 dpi, which is similar to an imagesetter. The significance of this is that it can actually produce the same halftone dots that film separations can. The colorants are printed onto a polyester page, which is laminated to the actual paper that will be used on press. The polyester acts as an intermediate page in this system.

Thermal transfer technology uses a print head that moves across the donor sheet, applying heat where colorant is required. The heat moves the colorant from the donor sheet to the substrate. The process is repeated for each color.

PIGMENT ABLATION

The final category of digital proofers is pigment ablation. Pigment ablation is a thermal transfer unit with a laser to transfer the colorant. As the name implies, it is a pigment-based system, but it works in a unique way. It has a RIP that controls dot gain, but it differs from most proofing machines in that it creates a tiny explosion in an aluminum layer in the colorant sheet that forces the pigment onto the paper in the image areas. The paper it can print on is limited to certain press papers.

PRESS PROOFS

Press proofs are the first printed sheets off a press — often part of the press check — which show how the final product will look. The press proof also shows what is on the plates and what should not be.

WHAT DO PRESS PROOFS CHECK FOR?

- Printing issues specific to the press being used.
- Trapping and registration of process colors.
- Dot gain.
- Moiré problems.

- They are printed on the press your job is actually printed on, using the actual inks and paper that will be used for the job. This will show the final visual result. It is exactly how your final job will look.

- Numerous proofs can be produced at a reasonable cost (after the first initial cost). These are often made for advertising agencies that require a number of proofs to distribute to customers.

HOW TO READ A PROOF

- Take your time; make sure you examine each page fully.

- Make a list of the features in the original document and check the proof against the list to ensure they are reproduced correctly.

- Look at the registration, trim and bleeds, type, color, overlays, tints, and gutters.

- Mark any flaws, blemishes, or anything else that seems wrong.

- Check and double check corrections made on previous proofs.

- Review the piece as a whole; is it clear and well presented?

- Ask about anything that you do not understand.

- If any changes need to be made, discuss the cost and who should pay for them.

- Mark corrections directly on the proof; be detailed and specific.

HOW TO CREATE YOUR OWN DESKTOP PROOFS

It is important to check proofs at all stages of the process. However, the desktop proof is one of the most critical. When you print your desktop proof make sure to print it at 100%, and turn on crop marks, printers marks, and registration. If the job is too large to print on your printer at 100%, tile the document. Tiling the document at 100% shows mistakes that may not be visible if you print a proof at "fit to page" instead of 100%.

Print out a composite print. This is the normal print you make from your desktop printer. Also print black-and-white separations, which will reveal any unwanted spot colors in the document, and determine if you properly overprinted or knocked out type.

CHAPTER 20

PAGE LAYOUT PROGRAMS

A page layout program can position pieces of a document into a page or pages. Programs such as Adobe InDesign and QuarkXPress allow you to import images and text into one program and arrange them in any order. This chapter covers how to use layout programs. It will help you to better use the tools available to you, as well as provide some pointers.

PAGE LAYOUT CAPABILITIES

One thing people seem to forget with page layout software is that you are not actually placing an image on the page. This means that you always need to have your original files included on the same disk or CD. If not, only the screen version of the file will print, not the original file itself. You can check the usage of fonts and images under Quark's Utilities>Usage tab.

> **NOTE:** Just because you *can* use all these techniques does not mean you *should*.

If the picture usage tab lists a file as missing, you can update that file and tell the program where it is now located. For example, if you rearranged some folders and moved some files around, the program may need you to tell it where they are now located.

The usage dialog box also permits font substitution. If you mistakenly used the stylized commands like **bold** or *italic* to mark text instead of the correct font, you can correct all instances of that in the font usage dialog box. For example, if you decide you do not want Helvetica in your document and want to change it to another font, you can change all occurrences of the font by clicking on the Replace button.

You can correct for the stylized fonts here. The three boxes in the bottom right corner (*P, B, I*) stand for plain, bold, and italic. Those words appear next to the font name in the font usage dialog box. If anything other than plain (P) is shown you are not using the correct font and it may cause problems in printing. Unclick the B or I box and replace the font with the correct bold or italic font.

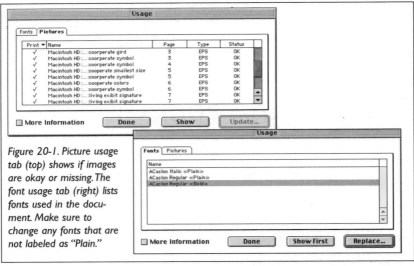

Figure 20-1. Picture usage tab (top) shows if images are okay or missing. The font usage tab (right) lists fonts used in the document. Make sure to change any fonts that are not labeled as "Plain."

JOB ORGANIZATION

It is a good habit to form folders at the start of a job. Make separate raster, vector, typeface, and layout folders before you start the job.

Figure 20-2. Organize your job folders. It makes the whole process easier if it is clear where everything is.

DOS AND DON'TS IN LAYOUT PROGRAMS

As discussed previously, layout programs try to be all-inclusive. However, there are many things that you should not use a layout program for in order to avoid causing problems later when a job is processed for printing; some features can slow down processing time and even crash a job.

IMAGE MANIPULATION

Never manipulate images or graphics in a layout program. A layout program assigns code to the final document, telling it to change the original image file; this creates longer RIP times and more chances for problems. The RIP will first create code for the image at 100% and then apply the layout modifications. As tempting as it may be to just change the number values in the tool-boxes, don't. Never scale, rotate, skew, or crop images within the layout program. If the project calls for these, go back to the original file in the vector or raster program and make your changes there. Resave the file and bring the new file into the layout program.

Also, never use white picture boxes as cropping devices in a layout program (or a vector program). The RIP still needs to process the whole image lying underneath that white box. This is also true in vector programs. Learn to use tools like scissors, which actually delete the unneeded portions instead of just hiding them.

NEVER USE THE HAIRLINE

Always define a specific width. A hairline is actually the width of one row of a printer element. These rows can vary from printer to printer and image-setter to imagesetter, so technically, you may never get the same hairline width twice.

| X: 1.403" | W: 5.972" | (△ 0°) | X%: (100%) | ◇◇ X+: 0" | (△ 0°) |
| Y: 1.111" | H: 4.076" | (△ 0) | Y%: (100%) | ◇ Y+: 0" | (△ 0) |

Figure 20-3. Never use the circled items. These values should always remain zero.

DON'T FORGET BLEEDS

If you plan a job to include a bleed, make sure to include it in your file. This does not mean you extend the image or background to the end of the page; you need to extend it past the edge of the page. The standard amount to extend a picture box beyond the page is 0.125 in. In QuarkXPress 4.0, you need to indicate the bleed measurement in the print dialog box. If you don't, you will not get a bleed on your image.

JOB SIZES

While we are talking about document sizes, let's not forget to mention job sizes. If your job is a custom size, for example, 11×13 in., specify that when you create the document. Do not use a tabloid-size document and create a smaller page layout within the tabloid page. This will cost more in prepress, and may cause problems for imposition software.

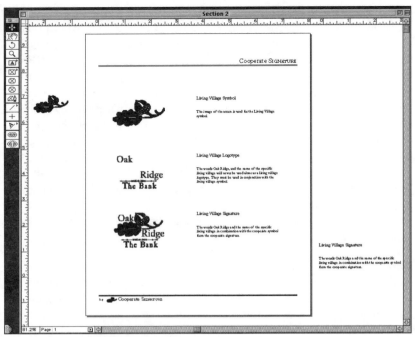

Figure 20-4. Items on the pasteboard should be deleted.

CLEAN UP YOUR DOCUMENT

Before you are finished, check your job to see if there are any unused image or text boxes outside the document (called the *pasteboard*). Make sure to delete them because they will only add to RIP time, which could cost more.

CHECK COLORS

Make sure your colors have the correct name. For example, if you are using a Pantone color in a graphic, make sure it has the exact same name if you are using the color in a layout program. 175 CVC is not the same as 175 or 175 PVC. Also, check what process you are printing in. Is the job CMYK or are you using spot colors? If you are printing in CMYK and you have spot colors in your document, you will have to change them and vice versa, unless the printing press you are using is capable of more than four color units.

COLLECTING FOR OUTPUT

In QuarkXPress and Adobe InDesign, you have an option to collect the pieces of the job for output. This feature is very useful for creating the final job package, which you will later deliver to a service bureau.

CHAPTER 21

MAKING PDF FILES
WITH ADOBE ACROBAT

Portable Document Format (PDF) is defined by Adobe as a file format used to represent a document independent of the application software, fonts, hardware, and the operating system used to create it. PDF files are self-reliant files that remain intact regardless of the platform they were created on. They can be moved electronically from computer to computer to be viewed or printed, and retain their content and format integrity. They are read using Adobe Acrobat Reader, and created using Adobe Acrobat Distiller or PDFWriter. More and more printers and service bureaus are using PDFs in their specific workflows. Check with your printer or service bureau for the settings that they prefer when using a PDF workflow.

THE IDEAL DIGITAL DOCUMENT

DESIGN RICHNESS

PDF has the ability to preserve design richness in documents from start to final output. PDF is able to properly reproduce all content information within a document, such as bitmap, vector line art, and text.

PORTABILITY

PDF files are portable across computer platforms, hardware, and operating systems. Documents can be exchanged without suffering from a lack of formatted text, loss of graphics, and lack of proper fonts. PDF is portable because it is a 7-bit (bit-depth is explained later in this chapter) ASCII file and is only able to use the printable subset of the ASCII set to describe documents, even documents with images or special characters.

NOTE: ASCII, The American Standard Code for Information Interchange, is the most basic coding system for text, and serves as the foundation for virtually every system that encodes information. Almost every document can be saved as ASCII, which can then be imported to any other document.

EDITABILITY

PDF files are editable because PDF is vector-based and includes the font name, character metrics, and style information of your text. Small, last-minute type changes can be made using a plug-in for Acrobat Exchange called Text Touchup. Full paragraphs cannot be edited due to the lack of reflow capabilities, but you can change a name or a spelling error if you need to.

PREDICTABILITY

PDF eliminates the variability of PostScript, on which it is based, and provides a foundation for effective digital print-production workflow. PostScript, a page description language, is interpreted by a RIP, converted into a display list of page objects, and rasterized into a map of on/off spots that tell the printer where to print the spots.

When your file is distilled into a PDF, the interpretation and display list functions are being completed as they would be in the RIP. The PDF file is a database of objects that appear on a page and how they relate to each other. A PDF file loses the variability of a PostScript file, but still maintains the essence of PostScript so that it can be printed. Your document will likely output reliably on most PostScript RIPs if it can be distilled into a PDF.

SEARCHABILITY

With PDF files you can find information instantly. Acrobat software offers a full-text search tool that allows you to retrieve the information you are looking for. Browsing and navigation features such as bookmarks can be simplified with hypertext links. Cross-documentation links can be included to help you move through various documents faster.

REPURPOSABILITY

Not only can PDF documents be printed, they are also used as a Web tool that offers greater design richness over HTML language constraints. PDFs can be uploaded to the Internet and accessed through Acrobat Reader, which can be downloaded free from the Adobe website.

HOW PDF FILES WORK

Although the portable document format is based on PostScript, it is not a programming language like PostScript. A PDF file cannot be sent directly to a laser printer because it contains information that a PostScript RIP would not understand. PDF files do contain PostScript code, but the extra data would keep the RIP from processing the document. A PDF file must be sent to a RIP through the Acrobat Reader, which converts the PDF file into a PostScript file and sends it to the RIP.

DEALING WITH FONTS

LEGAL ISSUES WITH EMBEDDED FONTS

Embedding fonts into a PDF file includes a compressed and encoded version of the font file, making it possible to illegally take the font information and use the font. Due to this, only certain vendors and type developers have given permission to embed their fonts in the file. Those who do allow font embedding in PDF files are:

- Adobe Type Library and Adobe Originals
- Linotype-Hell, AG (now Heidelberg)
- International Typeface Corporation (ITC)
- Agfa-Gevaert (which acquired Monotype)
- AlphaOmega
- Bigelow and Holmes
- Fundicion Tipografica Neufville

NOTE: If you are using fonts from another vendor, you may need permission for complete legal distribution of the fonts. You should check with the font vendor to be sure.

FONT EMBEDDING AND SUBSETTING

By embedding fonts in your document, you are placing an encoded, compressed version of the font in the PDF file. This allows your document to maintain its look and feel when turned into a PDF file. To embed a font in your PDF, the font file has to be available to Acrobat Distiller when you distill your document. You can either embed the whole font or a font subset. If you are planning to print your document you should embed the whole font to insure that the font is carried through the entire process, from application file to PDF.

Subsetting Fonts Embedding a font subset allows you to embed a version of the original font that contains only the characters that you used in your document. This is very useful because it allows you to embed fonts and reduce your file size at the same time. However, you cannot touch up text on a subsetted font if the characters are missing from those that you subset.

You can set a threshold for when to embed the font subset or when to embed the entire font, between 1 and 100%. In other words, if you set the threshold at 45% and you use 45% or less of a certain font, only the portion of the font that you used in your document will be embedded. If you use more than 45%, the entire font will be embedded in your document.

When you distill the file, it is important to note that the fonts must still be available to Distiller. The best way to ensure this is to embed all fonts into the PostScript file, or distill on the computer used to create the document.

Embedding Fonts To embed the fonts used in your document, you must either embed all fonts in the PostScript stream when you create your PostScript file, click the Embed All Fonts check box in the Fonts tab, or you must tell Acrobat Distiller where to look for the font files on your system in the Font Location folder. Once the fonts are located, you can embed them in the Fonts tab of the Job Options screen. (In order for Distiller to embed a TrueType font in a PDF file, the TrueType font must exist in the originating PostScript stream. You also must embed the TrueType font when you convert the PostScript file with Acrobat Distiller.)

Always/Never Embed List You have the option of designating specific fonts as always embedded or never embedded. This overrides any settings made to embed fonts or not. For instance, if you check the Embed All Fonts box and select certain fonts to never embed, the fonts in the Never Embed list will not be embedded. You have to make sure you have given the font location so that Distiller knows where to find fonts you want to always be embedded. If no location is given, fonts will not appear in the Always/Never Embed list unless they are the Base 14 Fonts or the fonts in your System folder.

UNDERSTANDING COMPRESSION IN PDF

Compression is a reduction in the size of a file by reducing the space required for storing the information in the file. There are various compression schemes, but most involve the removal of redundant data.

Graphic files take up huge volumes of space. As your file size grows, the need for RAM space to work on your image, as well as the need for space to store your files and time to process them increases, which is why compression is so important. Various compression options are provided in Acrobat Distiller.

COMPRESSION OPTIONS

For each type of image (color bitmap images, grayscale bitmap images, monochrome bitmap images), you have the option to downsample or sub-sample, which both discard unneeded data. If your image has an 800-ppi resolution and it only needs 400 ppi, downsampling or subsampling will get rid of the extra information in the image.

Subsampling evaluates the array of pixel data in your image and assigns a value for the entire area. The value of the center-most pixel in your image is given to the surrounding pixels. The rest of the data is thrown away.

Downsampling is similar to subsampling, but is more scientific in approach. Downsampling looks at the array of pixels in your image and averages the values; the average is assigned to the entire area. Both subsampling and downsampling have a minimum value of 9 dpi.

You can also choose a technique called *bi-cubic downsampling*, which is like downsampling, but uses a weighted average value to assign to the pixel area.

Subsampling does not produce as accurate a reproduction as downsampling; pixels are very noticeable when subsampling from high resolution to a very low resolution. The picture may look 'blocky.' Downsampling takes longer than subsampling, but the quality is better. Because pixels are averaged, the picture becomes fuzzier, but still looks better than subsampling. *Bi-cubic downsampling* is the most accurate method, but it takes longer to process the calculations. Bi-cubic downsampling is recommended because it is precise and results in the smoothest tonal gradations, although it takes longer to distill.

CHOOSING COMPRESSION

COLOR BITMAP IMAGES AND GRAYSCALE BITMAP IMAGES

Your next important decision is the type of compression you want to use. Compression is used to squeeze images into a smaller space, reducing file size. For both color and grayscale bitmap images you can choose *automatic*, *JPEG*, or *ZIP* compression.

Automatic Compression The automatic compression option in the Distiller software evaluates the images in your file and applies the appropriate compression scheme. This is usually determined by *bit depth*, or the amount of bits that are allocated for the description of each pixel of image data.

An 8-bit image has 8 bits of data to describe each pixel; an 8-bit image can rep-

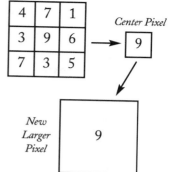

Subsampling

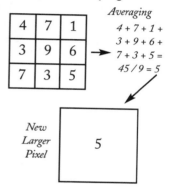

Average Downsampling

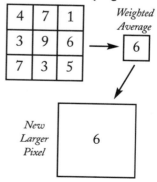

Bicubic Downsampling

Figure 21-1. Compression.

resent 256 colors (2^8). Each pixel in a 4-bit image can be represented by 16 different colors (2^4).

Images with smooth color changes, typically those with higher bit depths, have JPEG compression applied. Images with bit depth below 4, or with sharp color change, have ZIP compression applied. Automatic compression is not applied to line art, text, or monochrome images.

JPEG Compression JPEG (Joint Photographic Experts Group) compression is best used for images with smooth transitions between tones. These are typically images with higher bit depths. JPEG is designed to compress continuous-tone images, either in full-color or grayscale (black-and-white), and takes advantage of known limitations of human vision. The first areas in the image to be deleted are those containing small color shifts, and then areas of the next largest change are deleted.

For both automatic and JPEG compression, five levels of compression are available: minimum, low, medium, high, and maximum.

When you are using Automatic compression, the compression level selected applies only to files with JPEG compression automatically selected.

NOTE: As the resolution of an image increases, the effectiveness of JPEG compression increases because color transitions are smoother and there are more compressible areas.

ZIP Compression ZIP compression is best for images with sharp color changes, and can be applied in either 4-bit or 8-bit schemes. ZIP compression is best to use on line art, and is not recommended for continuous-tone images. ZIP achieves its highest level of effectiveness when applied to images with relatively large areas of single colors or repeating image patterns.

When ZIP compression is applied to color bitmap images you have additional control over the bit depth of the images in your file.

NOTE: If an 8-bit image is compressed with ZIP 4-bit compression, a loss of pixel depth will be the result.

MONOCHROME BITMAP IMAGES

The monochrome bitmap images section has similar menu items to color and grayscale images; Automatic compression is not available and the possible compression schemes are different. ZIP compression is available as well as CCITT Group 3 and 4, and Run-Length Encoding.

CCITT Group 3 and 4 The CCITT Group 3 and 4 compression techniques derive from facsimile transmission and are used on modern fax machines. This system converts the information in monochrome images into packets called *pels*, which are used in the description of the page. CCITT Group 3 and 4 can be very effective on pages that have good balance of black and white areas (in terms of percent page coverage).

Run-Length Encoding (RLE) RLE converts large sequential image data in a compressed form. It is best applied to large areas of black and white.

COMPRESSING TEXT AND LINE ART

To compress text and line art in your files, you simply click the check box at the bottom of the Compression tab. When you select this check box, text and line art are compressed with ZIP compression. No image data will be lost because this is a lossless compression technique.

LOSSY VS. LOSSLESS COMPRESSION

Lossy compression uses algorithms designed to compress the file by selectively removing portions of the images. The portions removed are details that the human eye does not pick out very well, so it usually does a good job of removing data. Some of the image information (detail) is lost in this method however, and artifacts or noise may be picked up in some images. The lossy techniques that are available in Acrobat Distiller when making your PDF are JPEG, subsampling, downsampling, and bi-cubic downsampling.

Lossless compression retains all pixel data for images and image integrity is retained. This type of compression is recommended for high-contrast images, line art, and text. Lossless compression techniques used for PDF files are ZIP, CCITT Group 3 and 4, and run-length encoding.

WORKING WITH COLOR IN PDF

Color management is the application of software to control the display and/or output of color on a variety of imaging devices so that the result of all device output matches the intended color representation. Settings made in the Color Tab will affect the final color of your design so proper settings must be made here. It is best to check with your printer or service bureau for the best settings to use with their color workflow.

COLOR OPTIONS

Preserve Overprint Settings These choices deals with overprinting images, either text or graphics, which are sometimes on a solid background. Checking this box makes it so all subsequent overprint settings are ignored. If you think there will be a need to have control over the overprint settings at the time your design is output, you should not make this selection.

Preserve Undercolor Removal and Black Generation Undercolor Removal (UCR) is the process of replacing a neutral shade composed of cyan, magenta, and yellow with a dot area of 70% or higher with a single black ink. Black Generation or Gray Component Replacement (GCR) is the process of replacing proportionate amounts of cyan, magenta, and yellow in areas of desaturated colors in a 10% dot or higher with black ink.

These techniques are used at the scanner workstation when creating a CMYK separation from an RGB scan, or can be made in a photo manipulation program such as Photoshop. UCR and GCR information is carried along with the PostScript file; you have the option of preserving or removing these settings. Preserving UCR and GCR keeps the settings intact and available when the file is sent to a specific output device that can handle the functions. Removing UCR and GCR by unchecking the box erases the function's associated information with the images.

TIP: UCR/GCR settings should be removed if the PDF is intended for electronic distribution. The settings should be preserved if the PDF is going to be printed.

Preserve Transfer Functions Transfer functions (or curves) are extra data for some images that is included in the PostScript code. This additional data is used when outputting your images to specific printers that support the use of these functions. These transfer functions can be preserved or removed. Removing the transfer functions may be the best choice for PDF files that you intend to use for electronic distribution because transfer functions are meant for specific output devices.

Preserve Halftone Screens It is important that you preserve halftone information for PDF files you intend to have printed. If you remove halftone screens, the default settings on the particular output device will be used. If you preserve the halftone screens you will be transferring your desired halftone screen information to your PDF file. The desired screen angles and shapes will be used when you print your PDF.

CHAPTER 22

DEALING WITH FILE FORMATS

Photos and graphics are stored, translated, and conveyed in a number of formats. It is important to understand the difference between a file format (PICT, EPS) and the types of graphics (bitmapped and vector) that applications produce, in order to appropriately save your files.

A file format is the structure of the data used to record information. The same data structure can be used to record more than one type of graphic, and a given type of graphic can be stored in several data structures. For example, a PICT file format can contain both bitmapped and vector graphics, and a bitmapped image can be stored in PICT, TIFF, or EPS format. Every combination of file format and graphic type has advantages and disadvantages.

GRAPHIC TYPES

There are two categories of graphic types: bitmap or raster, and vector.

THE BITMAP

The most basic type of graphic is the *bitmap*. It is essentially a grid of dots — a mosaic made from many tiny black-and-white or colored tiles, or bits. The tiles are called pixels, or picture elements. Lines are built up as rows of adjoining pixels, and all shapes are outlines filled with black and white, gray, or colored pixels. The optical illusion of colors that are not there is achieved by *dithering*, or mixing tiles of nearby colors or shades of gray. Dithering looks at the colors or grays in one row of tiles, and the colors or grays in an adjacent row, and then averages the two rows to create a third row in between.

Black-and-white bitmaps need only one bit to describe each pixel — zero or one. A single bit per pixel does not provide enough information to specify a color or shade of gray. Images containing 256 grays or colors require 8 bits per pixel; photographic-quality, full-color images require 24 bits per pixel to specify any of 16.7 million colors. Depending on resolution, color and grayscale, bitmaps require significant volumes of storage.

Bit Depth	Colors Available
1-bit	Black and white
4-bit	16 colors
8-bit	256 colors
16-bit	Thousands of colors
24-bit	Millions of colors

Printing a bitmap gives you only the resolution you started with. Low-resolution bitmaps print at low resolution, even on high-resolution output devices. If you print to a 2540-dpi imagesetter, that 300-dpi image looks terrible. Most professional systems only use bitmaps for photographic images.

THE VECTOR

Vector graphics, typically produced by drawing programs such as Adobe Illustrator or Macromedia FreeHand, overcome the limitations of bitmaps. The images are composed of mathematically described objects and paths called vectors. Vector applications store your strokes as a list of drawing instructions compiled from menu choices and mouse actions. Think of vectors as lots of electronic rubber bands that describe the outline of the image. Everything you draw, move, or change updates an internal file that lets the program keep precise track of each item in the drawing.

NOTE: Vector graphics are the natural choice for illustrations, line art, business graphics, and so on. Vector images have smooth curves, grayscale shadings, and tints.

You can enlarge, reduce, rotate, reshape, and refill objects, and the program will redraw them with no loss of quality. Moreover, you can manage objects as if each item were drawn on a separate transparent sheet. They are freely movable over the surface of a document and can be stacked and partially hidden by other objects without being permanently erased.

The advantages of vector art extend to the printing phase as well. Instead of dictating to the printer where each pixel should be, the program mathematically describes the object and lets the printer render the image at the highest resolution possible. Thus, unlike bitmaps, vector graphics are resolution-independent. A vector image printed on a 2540-dpi imagesetter looks far superior to the same object printed on a 300-dpi laser printer.

Line work (since it includes items with well-defined edges like text, rules, and logos) needs higher resolution to avoid stair-stepping. To merge the line work convincingly with bitmap data, not only does the spatial (i.e., scan) resolution have to be high, but the tonal resolution (i.e., bit depth) also has to match the continuous-tone scan. This results in a large line art file. As an example, a 300-dpi, 1-square-inch CMYK file requires about 350 KB of storage space. By increasing the resolution to 1,800 pixels per inch (about what a line work file requires), the file size increases by a factor of 36 to 12.4 MB. (An 8×10-in. file at that resolution would be a gigabyte in size.)

WHICH FILE FORMAT IS BEST FOR YOUR JOB?

Once you have created an image, how should you save it? There are many choices and each of them has distinct advantages and disadvantages. The trick is knowing the end use of the image. Will it be used on the Web? GIF and JPEG are the dominant Web file formats. Is it going to be imported into a page layout program? Then EPS or TIFF is the file format of choice. Depending on the end use of the image, there are specific file formats to use and those to stay away from.

You should continually save your document as you work. You never know when a computer will crash. While working on an image it is best to save it in its native file format until the end. For example, when working in Adobe Photoshop, save the images as .psd. That way you can save layers and, if needed, are able to make adjustments to them. When the image is complete, save it in another format if you need to. You should also save a final native file format version if space permits, in case changes need to be made to the original.

FILE FORMATS

Most imaging applications (like Photoshop) can import and export images in different formats. Image manipulation and publishing programs like QuarkXPress accept most file formats and save in an equal number of formats. Some programs also store images in a proprietary format, which contains specialized information that only the creating application can fully interpret. When a program converts an image from a proprietary to a generic format for export to other programs, some of the image's special attributes may be lost.

You can often identify a graphics file by its descriptor extension. DOS-based systems usually include it as part of the file name automatically; Mac systems tell you in the "Get Info" box. When working with Macs, get in the habit of putting a period and the three-letter extension that tells you what the format is. It helps to have an immediate knowledge of what you are dealing with. The following chart shows the major file formats used and a comparison of their features. Use this information when selecting which file format to use, based on the needs of the job.

	Mac	PC	Raster	Vector	1-Bit	2-Bit	4-Bit	8-Bit	16-Bit	24-Bit	32-Bit	Compression
TIFF	x	x	x		x	x	x	x	x	x	x	Yes
PICT	x		x		x	x	x	x	x	x	x	No
Photoshop	x	x	x		x	x	x	x	x	x	x	No
GIF	x	x	x		x	x	x	x				Yes
JPEG	x	x	x							x	x	Yes
EPS	x	x		x								No

JPEG

The Joint Photographic Experts Group (JPEG) was formed to create a standard for color and grayscale image compression. It is effective only on continuous-tone color spaces. JPEG describes not one but a variety of algorithms, each of which is targeted for a particular class of image applications. These algorithms fall into two classes: *lossy* and *lossless*.

Lossy refers to the compression method, which discards data that cannot be retrieved. Lossy compressed files are very small and are good for Web graphics, for example. Lossless is a compression method that does not lose any data when compressed, though the files are larger.

TIFF

Tagged Image File Format (TIFF) files are versatile bitmaps; this is the most commonly used method for storing bitmap images in various resolutions, gray levels, and colors. TIFF (now called TIFF/IT) does not store vector images; it was created specifically for storing grayscale images, and is the standard format for scanned images and photographs.

TIFF is a format for storing and interchanging raster (as opposed to vector) images — scanners, frame grabbers, and paint and photo-retouching programs. TIFF describes images in a number of formats and also supports several compression methods. It is not tied to proprietary products and is intended to be portable. It is designed so that it can evolve as new functions become necessary. Because TIFF had been designed to evolve, it was possible to create new tags for TIFF/IT to satisfy requirements of high-end systems. TIFF offers a compression option known as LZW.

LZW is designed to compress all kinds of data, including images of a variety of bit depths. LZW is lossless, which means that there is no loss of quality due to compression. However, for grayscale and full-color images (particularly those images with a lot of detail) LZW may not be able to offer significant amounts of compression.

LZW is an adaptive compression method, which means that the compression technique is dynamically adjusted based on the content of the data being compressed. LZW may also be termed a dictionary method of compression because it creates dictionaries, which are used to compress commonly repeated data.

CAUTION: LZW can unfortunately cause problems in high-end RIPs. While proofing and storing files, LZW is fine. However, save the TIFFs without LZW before going to the printer.

POSTSCRIPT

In the early 1980s, Adobe Systems, Inc. developed PostScript to improve text and graphic capabilities, and to control output devices including printers and imagesetters; it is the most commonly used page description language. PostScript uses a method to describe typographic images as vectors or outlines, thus allowing type to be infinitely modified and distorted. Most type had previously been bitmapped, which allowed no change in size or style.

A PostScript file is a purely text-based description of a page. In many applications, you can create a PostScript file from the Print dialog box. You can open that file with any word processor and modify it (if you know PostScript).

When you click the print command of any job, the page is converted to PostScript code and sent to the printer's RIP. You can save the page or document as a PostScript file — the same one that would have been sent to the printer — for later printing. You do not need the originating program to print a saved PostScript file; it can be fed directly to a PostScript printer with a PostScript download utility. Unfortunately, there is no preview image, and the graphic essentially loses its editability; always keep the original version of an image or a page in the native format of its originating application.

EPS (ENCAPSULATED POSTSCRIPT)

EPS is a PostScript file with a preview. It is used for storing vector and bitmap artwork. EPS has two subtypes: ASCII (text-based) and binary (hexadecimal). Vector programs (such as Adobe Illustrator and Macromedia FreeHand) that allow EPS often use the ASCII format.

An EPS file in ASCII format usually contains two versions of the graphic. One is a resolution-independent PostScript (text) description for printing on a PostScript device. The second is a low-resolution bitmap preview that can be displayed on the monitor without PostScript interpretation.

If a vector image is saved as an EPS, it will retain its resolution-independent printing quality and, in most cases, cannot be ungrouped, refilled, or re-colored. It can be resized, distorted, or cropped. Because EPS files are self-contained, most popular programs that perform color separation accept and color separate EPS files.

Binary EPS is similar to the ASCII version, containing both a bitmap preview image and the actual graphic. Instead of being a text-based description, the printable graphic is stored as a stream of numbers that represent the pixel attributes. Binary EPS is voluminous but well-suited for outputting bitmap color images for four-color separation. A binary EPS bitmap uses about half the disk space of its ASCII EPS counterpart. Many programs have a specific save option for binary EPS.

OPI (Open Prepress Interface)

OPI is an extension to PostScript that automatically replaces low-resolution placeholder images with high-resolution images. If you were to import a high-resolution picture into your document, the size of your document would increase astronomically. This especially becomes a problem if you are doing high-quality catalog or magazine work. Since picture files are usually large, just getting them from where they are scanned to your workstation can be a challenge if the place where they are scanned and sent to film is remote from the place where the pages are produced. Why not scan the picture and save the high-resolution version at the printing or prepress location, and create a low-resolution version to use for page makeup?

OPI is the solution to this problem. The low-resolution file is easy to handle and allows the page to be assembled with all elements in position. When the final file is sent to print, the OPI server replaces the low-resolution image with the high-resolution image. The only problem is that the images must remain unchanged. The image can be cropped, but cannot be manipulated.

DCS (Desktop Color Separation)

Where OPI works with TIFF images, DCS is a file format that creates four-color separations by saving images as a set of Encapsulated PostScript or EPS files. It is used to exchange color data between retouching, separation, and page layout programs.

The basic specification, which Quark, Inc. made freely available to other developers, includes five linked EPS files — CMYK separations and a composite master file that allows users to print low-resolution composite files on a color printer. This standard is called five-file EPS or EPS 5.

The advantage of DCS is that it allows an image-editing program to perform color separation and pass it through to final output with its integrity maintained. Users can choose which of several image editing programs or systems they want to use to create DCS separations independent of the final page creation and the separation of color elements on the page, such as type or line art.

The DCS format was adopted by Adobe Systems as a standard method of output for the first version of Adobe Photoshop. DCS provided a convenient way to prepare separations in Adobe Photoshop before rasterizing the PostScript file in a page layout program. This division of labor saved processing time, and a combination of Adobe Photoshop and QuarkXPress became popular among designers and prepress services for outputting pages with color images.

Users have said they wanted to see some reduction in DCS file size; DCS files contain bitmap data for each file of the CMYK separation, and most also include a complex, 8-bit, 72-dpi, four-color view file.

CHAPTER 23

THE RIP AND PREFLIGHTING

Once you have completed your files and passed them on to your printer or service bureau, it is necessary to make film or plates, or to print your file on a digital printer. In order to do this, your files must be sent through a RIP, which converts your files into printable dots.

HOW DOES THE RIP WORK?

When your files are sent to an imagesetter, platesetter, or printer, all of the data that makes up the file is converted into PostScript code.

A driver converts the pages that you design into PostScript code. The driver can be part of the system-level software or it can be built into some applications. Once your files have been converted into PostScript code, that code can be sent to the RIP. The RIP then interprets the PostScript into the output device's specific language, and a display list of the objects in the file is created. The display list is a simplified list of the PostScript code that tells the output device what it needs to draw on each page. The RIP then rasterizes the information in the display list, or determines every spot on the page in which a dot needs to be drawn.

WHERE DO YOU FIND THE RIP?

The RIP can be either software or hardware. *Software RIPs* can be purchased and installed on your desktop computer. Your computer's CPU, RAM, and storage are used to process PostScript and perform the function of the RIP. The interpretation instructions are contained in the software. This type of RIP is less expensive and easier to upgrade.

Hardware RIPs can be a chip placed inside a printer, such as a desktop laser printer, to perform all of the necessary functions; or a separate computer with its own motherboard, typically used for imagesetters. Hardware RIPs are a separate computer, like any other computer with RAM, storage, and ports. A PostScript processing chip, however, replaces the CPU chip.

Why You Need To Be Concerned With the RIP

PostScript seems like a precise page description language, yet there is always room for error. When your file is sent to a printer, imagesetter, or platesetter, the entire PostScript code must be interpreted and rasterized before anything can be printed. The more complex the PostScript, the longer it will take to RIP your files. Your files may not print at all.

As stated before, PostScript code must be converted into information that the output device understands before your design can be printed. PostScript has no restriction on the number of commands that can be used to describe a page, while the interpreter in the RIP works as fast as the speed and memory of the computer it is in. As a result, the RIP can take an extremely long time to process your files, or fail completely.

Throughout this book, many of the things that can go wrong and cause problems with the RIP are discussed, as well as solutions and the correct way to create your design. One of the goals of this book is to help you create printable files. The RIP is "picky," and things that you may not think of do make a difference. For instance, the type of fonts you use can have a major impact on your file's ability to be processed. Things done with vector and bitmap images can cause problems, as can the size of your file and its format. Leaving images in the wrong color mode or using too many spot colors can be irritating to the RIP. Simply rotating an image in a page layout program can slow down the RIP.

While the information in this book will help avoid problems with the RIP, many things can still go wrong, and it is best to ask your printer or service bureau what specific things you should avoid in your designs and for specific guidelines for setting up your files. Ask your printer or service bureau for a pre-flight checklist. If you have done everything according to your service bureau's specifications, you more than likely will not have problems with your file.

When you give your finished files to your printer or service bureau, they will almost certainly preflight (check your files to check for errors). You also have the option of preflighting your files before you give them to your print-er or service bureau; this can save you from having to pay your service bureau to fix mistakes. You can always fix these errors yourself after your printer or service bureau tells you about them, but the time it takes to fix your files could throw off the printing schedule and you would risk not getting your job printed in time.

WHAT IS PREFLIGHTING?

Preflighting is the process of checking electronic files to make sure that the necessary elements, including fonts and image/graphic files, are present, and that all of the necessary steps have been taken to make sure the file has been created correctly. Your printer or service bureau, on a more technical and involved level, will always preflight your files. It is important that a professional experienced in prepress issues check your file for mistakes. This person will know the intricacies of the process and the characteristics of the devices used. The prepress operator, for example, will know how your file will RIP, and what is necessary to fix errors.

There are various preflight software packages available if you wish to check your files ahead of time; this may save your printer or service bureau from any extra hassle, as well as save yourself money. Preflight programs alert you to problems, help you understand what they are, and explain possible ways to fix them. You can also use the programs to go through your files and fix problems item by item.

Before using preflight software, you should customize it to your printer or service bureau's specifications. Ask for a preflight checklist or a template for the particular software you are using. They may support that software and already have a template with the specific settings they would like you to use.

CHAPTER 24

ON-DEMAND AND
VARIABLE-DATA PRINTING

On-demand printing can be defined as printing a product as it is needed. On-demand printing prints and finishes the product. For example, as a book is ordered, it is printed, bound, finished, and sent to the customer.

Many large traditional publishers are using on-demand printing to print *backlist titles*, which are a publisher's available titles that were printed and released before the current season. With on-demand printing, these books can be printed for even one customer, if necessary.

Variable-data printing means that you can change the information (text or images) of a string of printed pieces. The data could be someone's name, address, numbers, or pictures of different cars. Variable-data printing is most often used for personalization of direct marketing materials.

A personalized letter is the most common example of variable-data printing used for direct marketing. For example, a credit card company may send a letter specifically directed to a potential customer telling them that they are eligible for a credit card with an interest rate and credit line specifically tailored to that person. Today, even information in the body of the letter can be changed for each person.

Personalization works by allowing you to specify areas of the document in which certain fields are inserted to receive the variable information from a database. The field in the document

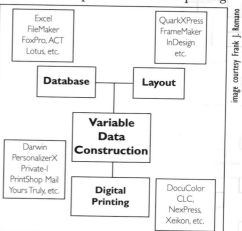

image courtesy Frank J. Romano

Figure 24-1. The Concept of Variable-data Printing. A database and layout are created and then combined in variable-data software. The merged database and layout are then printed on a digital press.

matches a field in the database. This tells the program to insert a record from the database into the appropriate field until each record has been applied. Images can be switched as well.

USING DIGITAL PRINTING

Digital printing is an integral component of the process for both on-demand and variable-data printing. With digital printing, each impression can be different because it does not use plates or static image carriers; the image is created on the image carrier for each impression. This is unlike conventional printing in which a fixed image carrier (a plate) is created and used to make each impression. In conventional printing, each impression will be exactly the same and usually requires hundreds of impressions to get one finished copy due to the process of getting the press up and running properly.

When a digital printer reaches a certain level of productivity it is called a digital press. There are four basic types of digital presses in current use: webfed dry toner, sheetfed dry toner, webfed liquid toner, and sheetfed liquid toner. Webfed refers to rolls of paper, while sheetfed refers to separate sheets of paper. Liquid-toner presses are currently only available from Indigo; all others are dry toner systems.

USING A VARIABLE-DATA WORKFLOW

Variable-data printing jobs typically follow a specific *workflow* (order in which the job is completed). The steps involved are:

1. A graphic designer is selected and hired, usually by the marketing manager of a company, to create a page layout. The graphic designer and marketing manager work together to select any variable images needed for the layout.

2. The graphic designer creates the layout using obvious placeholders for the variable data, including text and images. This layout is tested with the sample data that is obtained from the database administrator of the company, as well as a number of variable images. The designer creates proofs on a laser printer to be shown for approval.

3. A printer is selected. The designer, the designer's client, and the printer must communicate with each other to discuss the equipment and software that will be used to produce the variable-data print run. The designer must obtain any software or support files needed to transfer the job to the printer. It is especially important if the database needs to be manipulated for the specific job.

4. The designer transfers all files, including layout files, the database, images, and fonts, to a removable storage medium. A laser proof or folding dummy that indicates the layout and any folds, trim, or binding is included.

5. The printer runs a preflight operation, making sure that all necessary elements are included and the job is laid out properly for the specific press and imposition.

6. A digital press operator is assigned the variable print job. The press operator pulls a proof of the base document and submits it for client approval. The variable job is set up according to the software used once the proof is approved. It is then sent to the RIP and on to the press.

7. Once printed, the job is sent to be finished. It is cut, folded, and bound as needed. Any pieces that are flawed must be returned to the press operator to be reprinted.

DESIGNING A VARIABLE-DATA JOB

A personalized, variable-data job is created using one of the various software programs available. Most variable-data designs are done by creating the static information (that will be the same in every copy) in a page layout program such as QuarkXPress, and then creating the dynamic parts of the design (variable information) in a variable-data application such as Private I. The variable information can be text or images.

If you were creating a personalized poster in which the name and the meaning of the name changes on every copy, you would create the static information on the poster in QuarkXPress. For instance, the image or images on the poster would be positioned in the page layout program. Some variable-data programs require the static information to be saved in certain formats. Private I, for example, requires the page layout file to be saved as an EPS file.

In the variable-data application, the page layout file, saved in the required format, would be opened to access the text boxes for the variable information; in this

Figure 24-2. The variable fields are created in a variable-data application such as Private I and are enclosed in chevrons.

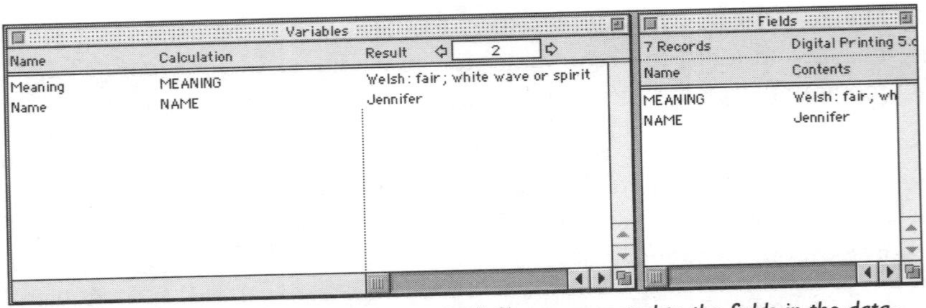

Figure 24-3. The variables created in the image (left) are connected to the fields in the database (right) by opening the database and dragging and dropping the variable field name in the image to the corresponding field in the database. The database fields are listed in the Fields dialog box on the right

case, the names and names' meaning of those receiving the poster would then be created and linked to the database containing this information. The text boxes for variables then need the name field typed in, typically enclosed in brackets or chevrons. «Name», for example, would be one of the fields (see Figure 24-2). Once the name field has been typed into the text box, it can be styled to enhance your design. You can select a font, font size, color, alignment, and so on.

When you are finished creating and styling the text boxes for the variables, the database is opened and the fields in your design are linked to the correct field in the database (Figure 24-3). This is the basic concept for variable-data design, but each program will work differently. You need to check with your printer and client to get the appropriate software and learn how to use it.

WARNING: To be sure there is enough room for the longest variable in the field, make the text box as wide as possible.

TEXT ISSUES

TEXT REFLOW

A problem specific to variable-data printing is text that overflows a variable-data text box. The overflow of the text may cause unsightly text breaks, or text may be missing completely. To avoid this problem, designers should create layouts and test them with sample data of the longest text string anticipated. Layouts should be printed to a PostScript laser printer and proofed to look for possible errors. Designers should make sure they have sample data to work with. Ask your client what the longest and shortest record might be, and test your design with those records.

OTHER TEXT TIPS

The resolution achievable with digital presses does not equal that of conventional presses. Digital presses do not clearly render type and fine artwork at small sizes. You should be aware of this when designing variable-data jobs, or any job that will be printed on a digital press, and take these tips into consideration:

- Do not set type smaller than 6 pt. or you will have difficulty seeing it.

- Do not set reversed type smaller than 9 pt.

- Avoid using a serif type under 12 pt. in reverse for digital printing.

- Typefaces with thin strokes do not reproduce well on digital presses unless they are used for display work in large point sizes. Didot, Bulmer, and Bodoni are examples of such typefaces.

- Typefaces such as Lucida, and the Stone and Utopia type families, were designed to be used on low-resolution devices like digital presses. However, these often look clunky in body text.

- Adobe Minion tends to look good printed on digital presses.

- Very thin lines in type or line art may disappear or look slightly jagged on curves. If you scan these, do so at the resolution of the digital press you plan to use. You should not resize or resample these. If you need a larger version, enlarge the type or line art on a photocopier and then scan it in.

DESIGN TIPS

Many of these tips are discussed at length in Chapter 5. They are relevant for variable-data jobs and any other job printed on a digital printer or press.

- The paper or other substrate you want to use must be approved for use in digital presses.

- The paper you choose has to withstand the high temperatures used to fuse the toner to the paper. Papers that do not meet the press manufacturer's specifications may crack, bubble, or resist toner deposit or adhesion; toner may flake off the sheet.

- It is a good idea to do a test run with the selected design, paper stock, and press.

- Toner may crack where paper is folded, so try to avoid placing images or areas with high toner coverage where you know the paper will be folded, especially on a cover.

- Coated paper can be glossy, dull, or matte. Toner used in digital presses may appear dull against glossy-coated paper; dull and matte-coated paper may look better because their dullness is close to toner. Digital printing looks great with uncoated paper.

- Some digital presses, such as the Xeikon, have an optional gloss-enhancing module (GEM). This polishes the fused toner, making it look very shiny; use this if that is the effect you want. Check with your printer for samples so you have a better idea what printed pieces that use the GEM unit look like.

- Variation in toner coverage may appear in large areas of solid color or screened tints, and blotchy areas may appear even in small areas when using screened tints.

CONSIDERING DIRECT-MAIL FORMATS

SELF-MAILERS

A self-mailer is a simple one-page design folded over once or twice, then mailed. They are typically printed on standard letter, legal, or A4 sheets of paper. They can simply be folded, or they can be folded and secured with tape or a glue dot. You may want to secure your design with tape to keep it in one piece while it is mailed.

When designing a self-mailer, keep in mind that it will be folded, and avoid putting a lot of toner coverage in the areas that will be folded. If there is too much coverage, the toner will crack.

There are also self-mailers with reply cards attached. This is when one of the folded panels is perforated and can be torn off and mailed back. It is important to select a paper that is sturdy enough to be sent through the high-speed sorting equipment used by the post office.

PACKETS

A packet is an envelope containing direct marketing materials. It is important to choose a light-weight paper that is sturdy enough to withstand the fusing process of digital printing, but light enough to keep postage costs down so that as much as possible can be included in the envelope. The envelopes used for packets typically use clear windows for the address information to show through, so make sure addresses line up in the envelope window.

POSTCARDS

Postcards can be many different sizes; however, they usually fall into two categories: 4.5×6-in. and smaller, or larger than 4.5×6-in. The smaller postcards can be mailed for just "post card" postage while getting first-class handling with no presort requirement. Anything larger than 4.5×6-in. requires full letter-size (first class) mail postage. Another option for both is using lower-standard mail rates if presort and mail preparation requirements are made and a permit is filed.

Make sure that the paper you choose is not too thin or it may not be mailable. Coated or uncoated stocks work as long as they are sturdy enough. Your best bet is to check with the post office.

BOOKLETS

Booklets are classified as anything folded over and saddle-stitched. As with any other area that will be folded, avoid large toner coverage or it will crack. You should also consider using a different substrate or paper for the cover. A booklet with the same paper for the cover and the inside, or a self-cover, is usually very flimsy and often meant to be read and then disposed.

Another consideration is whether or not to mail the booklet in an envelope. Without an envelope there is more chance of damage to the booklet. If you choose not to use envelopes, you should close the booklet with something such as sticky tabs or tape; staples are not recommended.

CHAPTER 25

WHAT HAPPENS AFTER THE FILE LEAVES YOUR HAND?

Once you have completed your design, it is ready to be sent to a printer or service bureau. What exactly happens then? First, you will most likely send your files on some sort of electronic media to the company's sales person or customer service representative (CSR), who is the person you contact with questions about your job. In fact, they should inform you of any specifics you need to know ahead of time, such as the applications that can be used and the versions, file formats, image formats, fonts that can be used, and so on. After you give your files to the customer service representative, they pass the files on to be preflighted.

PREFLIGHT

Preflighting, which is discussed in Chapter 23, is the process of checking your electronic files to make sure that the necessary elements, including font and image files are present. It also checks that the file has been prepared properly for the specific workflow used by the printing company. Most problems will be found at this point. Some of the most common problems are wrong or missing fonts, using spot colors instead of process colors, inadequate bleeds, sizing or rotating files in page layout programs, and not converting images from RGB to CMYK mode.

Once problems are found, your customer service representative will get in touch with you to see if you want the problems corrected by their prepress department, or if you want to correct them yourself. If corrections are made by the prepress department, the cost of your job will increase but this will save you time. To avoid these problems, check with your customer service provider before you begin your job and ask for a preflight checklist. Make sure your files have been created following their specifications. You can also use preflight software to check your files.

ESTIMATING, PLANNING, AND SCHEDULING

After corrections have been made and files have passed inspection, they are sent to the estimating department, which prices your job by taking into consideration any corrections made after preflighting. The planning and scheduling departments decide when your job will be printed. They also determine the specifics about paper, ink, and other resources needed for the job.

PREPRESS

TRAPPING

Steps such as trapping and imposition are taken care of in the prepress department. The type of *trapping* that you may deal with involves adjusting two adjacent colors that are different in order to avoid registration problems. *Misregistration* is when the objects look slightly out of place and white spaces show up on the printed page. Another type of trapping, wet and dry trapping, occurs on press and is not a direct design concern. *Wet trapping* describes how overprinting inks adhere to each other when wet ink is printed on top of wet ink. Each consecutive ink must adhere to previous ink(s) to produce the proper color. *Dry trapping* describes how overprinting inks adhere to each other when a coat of ink is overprinted on an already-dry ink.

Wet and dry trapping are not related to the topic of trapping as discussed in this chapter, but are included here so you will know the difference when talking to a printer.

Trapping is a necessary evil in the printing world. It is a simple concept, but one that is difficult to master. There are a few things you can do to trap your files, though it is recommended that you leave it to the professionals. If done incorrectly, it can just make things more complex and end up costing you more in the end. You should only trap if the file is a simple one.

The trapping you are more directly concerned with deals with knockouts. A *knockout* happens when you place an object of one color over an object of another color. In order for the color of the top object to print correctly, the top object must knockout the bottom object, leaving white space where the top object must print. If the different printing plates are printed in register, the top color will be printed perfectly in the white space. If there is misregistration, the top object will be slightly out of place and the color from the paper below will show through the gap that is created.

Spreads and chokes are used to create a trap and prevent problems caused by misregistration. A *spread* is the process of enlarging one of the objects slightly, and a *choke* is when you shrink one of the objects slightly. A spread is used if the overlapping image, such as a letter, is lighter than the background. The lighter colored letter will be spread out to slightly overlap the background. Chokes are used if the top image is darker than the background. If you put a dark letter over a light background, the knockout in the background is choked, or reduced slightly so that the dark letter would overlap the background a little.

Figure 25-1. If you place one color over another, the top object knocks a hole in the bottom object so it prints on white paper instead of the bottom color (left). The knockout prevents the color of the top object from changing.

To prevent problems with trapping, you can use techniques that avoid the need for knockouts. If you have text over a different background color, one possibility is to create white outlines around your text. This keeps the two colors from touching and prevents the need for trapping. Another possibility is to just overprint the different color images. *Overprinting* prints the overlapping image without knocking out the color beneath. As stated earlier, this will change the colors of the overprinted objects, but it will prevent any gaps from misregistration.

If there are problems with trapping, misregistration will occur, leaving a white gap between colors when they do not line up (right).

Figure 25-2. The left image shows a spread, in which the top (usually lighter) color spreads out into the darker background color. The right image shows a choke, in which the bottom (usually lighter) color is choked slightly to reduce the knockout and allow the top (darker) color to overlap without misregistration.

Figure 25-3. The Difference Between a Knockout (left) and an Overprint (right).

Should you deal with trapping? It is not recommended. Ask your printer or service bureau if they want you to set the traps in your files. They will most likely advise you not to. It is better to leave trapping to a professional.

If you trap within the application, do it as early in the process as possible. You may not be able to do it later and if it must be done, you will have to return to the first file to do it. For instance, if you import an Illustrator drawing into your QuarkXPress file, you cannot use the QuarkXPress tools to trap objects in the drawing. You must perform the trapping within the original Illustrator file.

BASIC TRAPPING GUIDELINES

- Use black or dark colors for very small or narrow items and specify them to overprint.

- *Overprinting* makes sure that light colored items are not created in knockout areas in dark backgrounds. These are difficult to trap and fill. Overprinting means that an image or color *prints over* the colors in the background instead of using trapping options.

> **NOTE:** Lighter colors are called subordinate colors and should be spread into darker colors called dominant colors.

- *Knockout* means that the program tells the RIP to leave out the color information at the indicated point. For example, if you have white text on top of a red background, you want the red to knockout where the white text is.

- If unsure about trapping values, talk to the printer.

- In order to ensure proper trapping, make proofs. Only those made by the printer may show traps.

IMPOSITION

Imposition is the process of arranging the pages of your design in the proper order on the printing plates or imaging cylinder so when they are printed and folded, they will appear in the correct order. (More information on imposition is found in Chapter 9.) The imposition of a job depends on many things, including the way your design will be bound. Again, talk to your printer or service provider, but most likely they will tell you not to worry about imposition. If they do want you to deal with imposition or trapping, it is best to ask them for directions on how to proceed.

CREATING A PROOF

After trapping and imposition, the prepress department will RIP your files and make a proof. At this point there should not be any errors, but if there are it is important to find them before plates are made. (Proofing is discussed in more detail in Chapter 19.) If mistakes are found, your CSR will contact you to discuss options for correction. Once a satisfactory proof has been made and you have signed off on the job, the prepress department will continue with the process and make plates.

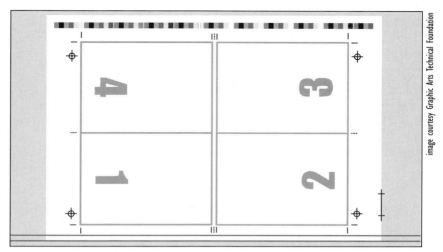

Figure 25-4. Imposition of a Job on a Printing Plate.

FILM AND PLATES

The prepress department will output films from your files, then create plates from those films. Or they will use newer technology and create plates directly from your files; this requires your job to be sent through a RIP (discussed in Chapter 23), and is why preflighting your files is so important.

If your job is being printed on a digital press, the process of creating film and plates is skipped and your files are sent directly to the digital press operator. Because digital presses use re-imageable carriers or inkjet ink and do not require printing plates, your job is printed directly from your files. Files are then archived and the plates or the files are given to the press operators.

PRINTING

Press operators will mount the plates, whether they are plates for lithography or flexography, or cylinders for gravure, and print your job. Once the job has been printed and approved, it is sent to be finished.

FINISHING

Your job will be finished at your printer's in-house finishing department, or it may be sent out to a company that specializes in finishing. The print job will be cut, folded, trimmed, stitched, or bound.

DISTRIBUTION

The finished product is then shipped to you or the customer who hired you to design the job. It is up to you or the customer who hired you to distribute the final product.

CHAPTER 26

WHAT TO ASK YOUR PRINTER AND WHY TO ASK IT

If you have questions, make sure you ask them. If you are unsure about a color conversion, a design idea, concept, or other element, discuss it with your service provider. They may be able to provide options you had not considered. Know what the printer needs from you and what you need from the printer. You and the printer are allies working together to make clients happy.

WHAT ARE THE PRINTER'S CAPABILITIES AND REQUIREMENTS?

MINIMUM AND MAXIMUM PRINT AREA
You need to find out the minimum and maximum paper size in order to design a printable piece. Be sure to find out how much space to leave for crop, trim, and registration marks.

PAPER GRAIN
Remember the paper grain when designing your folds and layout. Paper sheets can be cut grain-long or grain-short, so make sure the paper you order is correct for your job.

PRESS LIMITATIONS
Ask if there are specific limitations to the process you want to use.

LINE SCREEN
Since you will need to scan images at twice the line screen, find out the printer's preferred lines per inch (lpi). You only need resolution that is twice the lines per inch used on press. Any more than that and you will flood the computer and clog the RIP. Find this out before you even start to generate scans and make sure to have no more and no less than you need. Remember that it has to be twice the line screen at the final size, not just scanned at that resolution and then resized up.

Gradients

If you intend to use gradients in your file, ask what length of gradient you can use without banding, the degree of change from light to dark needed, and whether you can use gradient meshes.

Color Units

Find out the minimum and maximum number of colors the press can print in one pass. Printing the piece in two passes will increase cost and increase the chance for hazards such as misregistration. This will determine how many spot colors you can use economically and quickly.

Color Management

Find out what generic RGB or CMYK settings the printer prefers. Ask if you should convert to CMYK, or leave that to the prepress provider. If you are going to convert, ask for values they need to generate the best print possible. If you include any color profiles with the job, use a consistent naming convention that includes the date the profile was made.

File Formats

Certain file formats are used as part of a printer's workflow; make sure to find out what formats they prefer. If they use a PDF workflow, be sure to ask what job settings you should use; and find out if they have a saved Job Settings file to send you. For print, you probably do not want any compression options checked. If the job is going through an imagesetter, you may need to set the resolution very high. Make sure to save the right version (3.x, 4.x, 5.x). If you are using spot colors, be sure to save the file in a way that maintains them. Adobe InDesign lets you use file formats that will be rejected at the RIP, including PSD, JPEG, and native file formats; be sure to save those files as TIFF, EPS, or PDF.

Programs and Versions

It is important to find out the program capabilities of your printer to avoid sending a file they are unable to open. Send files saved in the right version of the program. Most printers have the most recent version of software, but it is better to check ahead.

Storage Media

Find out what method of delivery the printer prefers. Some places require electronic distribution, others require a burned CD. Zip and CD drives have become relatively standard, but you might want to ask before you send a Jaz, SyQuest, or Orb drive. Write your name and phone number on the disk.

HOW SHOULD YOU ORGANIZE FILES?

NAMING CONVENTIONS

Include extensions at the end of file names. Use short but memorable names. For example, "Document 1" is not a good name. Service providers, RIPs, and the Windows operating system may get frustrated by long names. Keep names simple, clear, and within the specifications of your printer.

ORGANIZE JOB FOLDERS

Ask if the printer has a specific way for you to name your file to make it easier to find what is needed during preflight. Group items in folders, and double-check links to make sure the master document can find all the pieces in the folders. One good idea is to start with the folders in place from the beginning, so you do not have to update everything at the end. Make your vector folder, bitmap folder, mechanical folder, fonts folder, and any other necessary folders and put all those, along with your layout file, inside a job folder. Collect for Output catches most of the pieces, but may miss fonts in embedded EPS files. If you have the images in a single folder, they are easy to access during troubleshooting and preflight.

HOW DO YOU CUT COSTS OR SPEED PRODUCTION?

SERVICE PROVIDER SUGGESTIONS

Discuss your ideas with your service provider; they may provide solutions that can save money. They can tell you what to avoid in the beginning to cut cost later on, what ideas would be costly, and simple solutions. They may suggest things like house papers, colors that are cheaper to print, or solutions to binding problems.

CALL THE BINDER AT THE BEGINNING

If your printer does not do in-house binding, remember to call a bindery to double-check for binding issues.

WHAT WILL CHANGES COST?

There will be charges for last minute editorial changes. Check to see how much correcting your file will cost once it is preflighted. An error caught on press will cost much more than an error caught on a proof.

TYPES OF CHANGES

Once the job has been handed off to the service provider, different changes may cost different amounts. A typographical error, for example, is on one plate; other changes may require a whole new set of films and/or plates. Slight color changes like saturating or desaturating one color are somewhat possible on press, but editorial changes are not possible: you would not be able to change a red dress to a blue dress once the item is on plate, but you might be able to make the red a bit more intense.

WHAT DOES THE PRINTER DO OR SEND OUT?

BINDERY

The print job is sent out to a bindery for coatings, binding, and print finishing (embossing, diecutting, folding). Some commercial printers do it all, many do not. If not, it means another person you need to contact and discuss your project with. Check with your bindery to make sure the idea will work, and that you are taking the necessary steps to make it work. Different departments within the graphic arts industry have different specialties. When you are trying to avoid problems it is important to work with people who are most familiar with the process.

HOW LONG WILL THE PROCESS TAKE?

COMPLEXITY OF THE JOB

Colors used, pages, signatures, folds, embossing, diecutting, coatings, bleeds and trims, large file sizes, and complicated graphics all may slow down the printing process.

SCHEDULING AT YOUR END AND AT THE PRINTER

Ask for the latest date you can turn the job in and still get it back when you need it, then aim to beat that date. Printers often schedule jobs in advance; find out when you have to give them the job so it fits both your schedules. If you turn a job in five days before you need it, but the printer has four big jobs ahead of you, you may not get your job in time.

How much time is needed for the printing process you want to use? If a printer has to make film and plates, mount them, and run the press to achieve correct ink/water balance, it will take time. If, however, you are using a digital press it may take a few hours. Consider the printing process, and find out how much lead time the printer needs to return the job to you.

DRYING TIME AND FINISHING

Often, the ink may need time to dry before it can endure a folding machine or trimmer. Any finishing will take time, especially if the printer has to send it to a bindery. Many times the ink has to dry before the job can be finished.

CHOOSING THE
RIGHT EQUIPMENT

Desktop computing involves so many components that choosing output devices, storage devices, and even the computer can be confusing. The components you select for desktop computing basically come down to preference, but many people feel there are advantages to certain devices.

SELECTING A COMPUTER: MAC VS. PC

The first choice to make is the type of computer. The computer contains the motherboard, the CPU, and the accompanying electronics, into which are plugged various logic boards, external connectors, disk drives, keyboards, a mouse, and so on. The *motherboard* is the circuit board that peripherals and other computer components are plugged into, through which data is transmitted and received. The central processing unit (CPU), is the main chip used to manipulate and process data. It is the brain of the computer.

There are two popular choices of computer platform, Mac or PC (personal computer). The word platform refers to the microprocessor the system uses, or the CPU. Mac computers use Motorola chips, while PCs use Intel chips. Both Motorola and Intel chips typically have numbers used to name them. As Figure A-1 shows, microprocessors become more powerful by integrating higher numbers of transistors, the building blocks of computer processors. Today, the newest microprocessors commonly used are the Intel Pentium in PCs and the Motorola Power PC in Macs.

In addition to different CPUs, Macs and PCs use different *operating systems*. The operating system is what allows the operator to control the computer. The operating system maintains the flow of information from disk to computer and back again, to disk and then monitor, from keyboard or other input device to disk, to printer or other output device from disk, and so on. Basic tools such as booting (turning the computer on), launching applications, file naming, copying, and accessing peripherals such as monitors, drives, and scanners are controlled by the operating system.

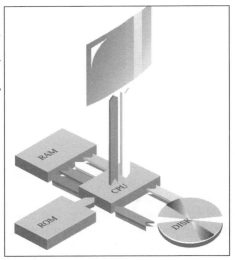

Figure A-1. Microprocessors become more powerful by integrating higher numbers of transistors.

The *graphical user interface* (GUI) is the way information is shown on screen, and is the interface used by the operating system to get things done. It includes the icons or pictures, menus, and functions that allow easy use of the system. The GUI allows users to simply click on icons to select a file or application, or point and click on menu items rather than type in commands the way computing was done in the past. Mac and PC platforms also have different GUIs.

Mac computers tend to be the choice of professionals in creative markets, including graphic design, corporate design departments, ad agencies, book and magazine publishers, catalog publishers, commercial photographers, and illustrators. This is most likely because Macs started as a graphical user environment, while PCs started with the DOS character-based environment. As a result, there is often the perception that Macs are good to use for graphics and PCs are good to use for computing numbers. That is the most likely explanation why Macs tend to be used for creative professions such as design and PCs tend to be used for business; however, today's Macs and PCs are capable of both types of computing.

There are many arguments about why one is better than the other, yet there is no clear answer. Some of the main comparisons between Macs and PCs deal with the CPU, ease of use, cost, and choice.

CENTRAL PROCESSING UNIT (CPU)

The CPU, as discussed earlier, is the brain of the computer. Macs and PCs use different chips for their CPUs, but it is difficult to determine which type of chip is actually better. Today's Macs and PCs are typically comparable in power and speed. Though many people use megahertz to determine the power of a processor, that only refers to the number of cycles a chip can complete in a given amount of time. Megahertz does not truly tell you how fast a computer is because it does not tell you how much information is being processed by each cycle of the chip.

Ease of Use

An argument in favor of Mac when comparing the two computers is ease of use. Mac's operating system is thought to be more intuitive than a PC and the Mac interface seems to be simpler to use and understand. Setting up a Mac is also considered easier than setting up a PC.

Cost

PCs are the choice when cost is the issue. There is so much competition in the PC market that the cost has been driven down. In general, you can find a PC system with a monitor, printer, modem, and software that is comparable to a Mac system's power and speed for less money.

Choice

In addition to costing less, PCs offer greater choice of brand: many companies sell them. If you want a Mac, you have to buy an Apple Macintosh; you do not really have the option of shopping around. Ultimately, the computer that you are most comfortable using is the best. It is also wise to contact your printer or service bureau to see what type of files they accept. They may use Mac and not be able to accept files created on a PC.

CHOOSING A STORAGE SYSTEM

You will need to save any work done on your computer. You can save it on your hard drive, or you can put it on some type of removable storage media. Removable media function either as a way to back up files saved on your hard drive, or to transport your files to another computer. As a designer, you will need to transport your files to your service provider.

In addition to the traditional floppy disk that most computer users are familiar with, there are various alternatives. The most common disk/storage systems in use are the Zip disk, CD-ROM, and DVD.

Zip Drives

Zip drives are very popular in the graphic communications industry, and are often a good choice for storing large publication and graphic files. *Zip disks* are 3.5-in. disks that are slightly thicker than floppy disks. They hold 100 MB of information, and are available for both the Mac and PC platforms. A 250-MB Zip drive has been developed, but has not been widely adopted. Zip disks are read-and-write, allowing files to be saved, deleted, and reused. You can get them as external drives, or as an internal drive that fits in a 3.5-in. drive bay.

Similar to the Zip drive, but used less frequently, are the Jaz and Orb drives. Jaz drives can hold 1 or 2 GB and Orb drives hold 2 GB. Both the Jaz and Orb are essentially hard drives with removable disk cartridges. All three of these drives are magnet based, and data that is stored magnetically can be disrupted easily by moderate electrical and magnetic fields.

CD DRIVES

CDs can be used for storage, backup, and easy transfer of files between computers. There are three main types of CDs:

- *CD-ROM*   Compact Disk Read-Only-Memory

- *CD-R*   Compact Disk Recordable

- *CD-RW*   Compact Disk Re-Writable

CD-ROM drives are only able to read information that has been previously burned onto the disk. This is convenient if you only want to look at a file or install software on your computer, but if you want to save a file that you created, you will need a CD-R or CD-RW drive. CD-R disks allow you to read files and to burn files to the CD-R disk once. You cannot, however, erase the files and use the disk again because the image is etched in the surface of the disk.

CD-RW disks allow you to use a disk over again. You can read files, burn files to the CD, erase the files, and burn new files to the disk because data is only smudged on the surface of a disk. Since the data is only smudged on the surface, it is possible that you can lose data, so CD-R disks are recommended for archiving your files after you have finished a job.

An advantage to using CDs for storage is that they are an optical storage device; they are unlikely to be damaged and do not wear out after constant use as do magnetic storage devices. If they are not cracked or scratched, they can last for decades. Again, remember that CD-R disks are your safest choice for long-term storage or archiving, while CD-RW disks are best for short-term storage and transporting data.

CDs tend to be fairly inexpensive and can hold 650–700 MB of data. CD-R and CD-RW drives are, however, somewhat expensive. CD-ROM drives typically come with computers today, but to make the most of CDs, you probably want a CD-RW drive.

DVD

The DVD drive is similar to the CD. It is an optical storage device; however, the tracks burned into the disk are narrower, allowing more data to be stored. The largest version of the DVD-ROM can hold up to 17 GB of data. DVDs come in read-only-memory, recordable, or rewritable formats. DVD drives are starting to gain acceptance and will most likely take the place of CDs at some point. Most DVD drives can read both CDs and DVDs.

PICKING DESKTOP PRINTERS

INKJET PRINTERS

Inkjet printing is a method in which ink droplets are sprayed onto paper as it moves through the printer. There are various types of inkjet printing, such as inkjet printing and bubble jet technology. There are also different methods for controlling the placement of ink on paper. In continuous printing, the spray of ink is controlled by electronic deflectors; drop-on-demand printing only sprays the ink as it is needed.

Lower-end inkjet printers are quite inexpensive, usually less expensive than laser printers. They have become more sophisticated and are able to produce good-looking illustrations and images. Images can look almost like photographs when printed on special glossy papers. Inkjet printers are also small and lightweight, making them a convenient choice for a desktop printer.

Inkjet printers do have disadvantages, however. They are often slow and take quite a while to print images. The color in images may also not look as nice if not printed on glossy paper. Some inkjet printers may have problems printing text as well.

LASER PRINTERS

Laser printers use toner to create image areas on paper and work in much the same way as a photocopier. A negative charge is created on the drum of a laser printer by the laser beam. The toner, a powder substance that can be either liquid or dry, in black, cyan, magenta, or yellow, is attracted to the remaining areas on the drum that have a positive charge. The toner in the positive areas is passed to the paper as it passes through the printer. Heat is used to melt the toner and fix it on the paper.

Laser printers have become more and more sophisticated. They work much like an office copier and are now able to print on two sides of the paper, collate, and staple; however, they create originals rather than copies. Laser printers are also very fast and more than one person at a time can send jobs to them. Laser printers are expensive. The quality of images produced by laser printers is not necessarily as good as inkjet printers, especially inkjet images printed on glossy paper.

LOOKING AT SCANNERS

There are many different scanners available. Most people have inexpensive scanners for scanning family pictures to use on their web site. For printing, you may want to have your scans done professionally. Alternatively, invest in a higher-quality desktop scanner. Once you make this investment, you should also invest in profiling equipment. Many higher-quality scanners are

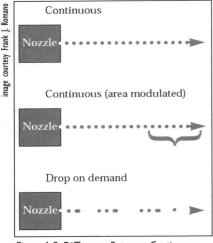

Continuous

Nozzle ∙∙∙∙∙∙∙∙∙∙∙∙∙∙∙➤

Continuous (area modulated)

Nozzle ∙∙∙∙∙∙∙∙∙∙∙∙∙➤

Drop on demand

Nozzle∙ ∙● ∙●● ∙ ➤

Figure A-2. Difference Between Continuous Printing and Drop-on-demand Printing.

equipped to self-calibrate; check with your scanner manufacturer to find out if that is the case with your scanner. If not, they may have a calibration system you can use.

Cheaper scanners have a limited capacity to record information; most can truly only scan around 600 samples per inch (spi). The box and the manufacturer may manipulate the description to make it sound more impressive, for example, promising that three RGB colors × the length of the glass × the width of the glass, all interpolated by software, "give you an amazing 4800 dpi!"

As scanners go up in price, their ability to see more detail, especially in the shadows, increases. A high-end drum scanner, even at desktop size, is very expensive, and can scan 4,000 spots per inch or more. If you need professional quality, have a professional do the work. A prepress house would typically give you a file that has a lower-resolution version of the scan for use in creating comps and layouts, and then provide the higher-resolution image to the commercial printer.

SELECTING A MONITOR

There are two types of monitors to choose from, cathode-ray tube (CRT) monitors and liquid-crystal display (LCD) monitors. These are based on different technologies and many people feel the LCD monitor is a better choice; however, there are advantages to CRT monitors.

LCD monitors are compact and lightweight, have a thin screen, and are used for laptops and handheld computers. CRT monitors use a tube and take up more space than LCD monitors. The display size, or screen height and width, is not a real issue anymore because LCD monitors are now available comparable in size to CRT monitors.

The display characteristics (colors, brightness, resolution, and viewing angle) do have differences and should be taken into consideration. CRT monitors typically are capable of unlimited colors at 14 inches and above. Newer LCD monitors are capable of unlimited colors, but many are only able to show thousands of colors. CRT monitors are generally very bright, while LCD monitors are backlit and not as bright as CRT. As newer LCD monitors are being developed, they are becoming comparable to CRT monitors.

Resolution is another consideration when buying a monitor. Monitor resolution is based on the number of pixels per inch in the monitor. The *pixel* is the smallest element that makes up the picture on the screen. As the pixel size gets smaller, more pixels make up the picture, giving it a higher resolution. Pixel size is based on *dot pitch* (DP); the lower the number, the higher the resolution. It is not recommended to get a monitor with a dot pitch above 0.28, or your monitor will start to look fuzzy. The resolution of CRT and LCD monitors are comparable for monitors above 14 inches.

Viewing angle is another concern when choosing a monitor. CRT monitors have a much larger viewing angle than LCD monitors. You can view a CRT screen from the side, while an LCD monitor has a smaller viewing angle and needs to be viewed from the front to see the screen clearly. This becomes a factor when using the screen for soft proofing (see Chapter 18).

Another important consideration when buying a monitor is price. CRT monitors have the advantage here. Smaller LCD monitors can be expensive, while larger CRT monitors can be found for much less.

LINKING TO THE PERIPHERAL WORLD

In order for you to use peripherals with your computer (a printer, scanner, or modem), your computer needs a way to connect them. There are various standards for connecting peripherals.

SMALL-COMPUTER SYSTEMS INTERFACE (SCSI)

SCSI, pronounced "skuzzy," allows seven to fifteen peripherals to be hooked to your computer at one time. Peripherals that can be connected are typically tape drives, hard drives, CD-ROMs, and scanners. An advantage to SCSI is speed. It can transfer 10–40 MB of data per second. A disadvantage is that users frequently risk corrupting their hard disks if they turn printers and scanners on or off after start up, or disconnect cables while the power is on.

UNIVERSAL SERIAL BUS (USB)

USB is a new way to connect peripheral devices to computers. USB gives a single, standardized, simple way to connect devices to computers. Up to one hundred twenty-seven devices can be connected at one time, giving it an advantage compared to SCSI. USB does, however, only transmit data at 1.5 or 12 MB per second, which is considerably slower than SCSI.

USB accepts many types of peripherals, such as keyboards, modems, printers, scanners, monitors, CD-ROM drives, and digital cameras. USBs are hot-swappable and hot-pluggable, making connecting a peripheral as simple as finding the USB port and plugging it in. You do not have to shut down your computer every time you want to connect or disconnect a peripheral.

FireWire

FireWire allows for faster transfer of data, up to 400 MB per second, and is expected to replace SCSI. FireWire can attach up to sixty-three devices and is hot-pluggable like USB, so you do not have to shut down your computer every time you want to connect or disconnect a device. One important advantage to FireWire is that in addition to computer peripherals, digital home entertainment devices such as digital camcorders, VCRs, and TVs can be connected. This is ideal for people who want to make their own videos.

NETWORKING

Networking allows you to move information from computer to computer without having to use some sort of removable storage media. A *local area network* (LAN) is a group of computers, printers, and workstations located within a defined area and connected together to share information and functionality. The LAN only connects computers within a room or building. A LAN transmits data at 2–10 million bits per second. Typically data is transmitted through physical cable or electronic transmission. There are also *wide area networks* (WAN) that connect workstations over a wider area; for example, a college may have a network that allows you to access the library server from a dorm room.

Typically a network card is needed to connect the computers, or nodes, to a network. Mac computers, however, come with an integrated network port called AppleTalk or Ethernet. All of the computers connected to a network are connected to a server, or central source of information available for use by workstations on the LAN. There are various types of servers, such as a file server, which allow users access to files that are stored on the server.

a* (a-star)

Axis in the LAB color space; encompasses green (−128) at one end and red (+127) at the other

Absolute Colorimetric

Rendering intent in which the white point of the paper is not factored in

Additive Color

When additive primaries are mixed, you see yellow, magenta, and cyan. Since you start with black (darkness) and add light in order to see color, RGB is considered an additive color space

Adobe Type Manager (ATM)

Font management program

Alphanumeric Character Set

Another term for a family of typefaces

Amplitude Modulated (AM) Screening

Conventional screening method in which halftone dots on film or a printing plate are created at a constant angle and number per inch. Dots of varying size create the illusion of dark and light tones

Analog proofs

Proofs made from film separations

Area Array

Sensor grid in a digital camera that captures the scene in one quick moment. Generally cheaper than linear-array cameras

b* (b-star)

Axis in the LAB color space, encompasses blue (−128) and yellow (+127)

Backlist Titles

Publisher's available titles that were printed and released before the current season

Basis Weight

Weight in pounds of a ream of paper (500 sheets) cut to a standard size

Bi-cubic Downsampling

Assigns a weighted average value to the pixel area

Bitmap Fonts

Fonts created from either black or white image pixels

Bleed

Anywhere that the color, image, or text extends (intentionally) past the edge of the page

Bluelines

Analog proof still used by many people, made by exposing a light-sensitive paper through the film. Good for mock-ups because they can be easily folded and bound

Booklets

Anything that is folded over and saddle-stitched

Calendering

When the paper passes through steel rollers to give it a certain finish without adding a coating

Calibration

Taking a piece of equipment and altering its behavior so that it is consistent

Case or Edition Binding

Most common type of binding for hardcover books, involves sewing the individual signatures together, flattening the spine, applying endsheets and a strip of cloth to the spine

Cathode Ray Tube

Big, boxy monitors that have light that shines through filters; these contain phosphors that deteriorate over time

Charge-Coupled Devices (CCD)

CCDs receive light that either bounces off reflective paper, or through transparent film. Most desktop scanners and digital cameras have tri-linear arrays, meaning that in one pass, the information from the red, green, and blue channels is recorded and stored digitally

Choke

Used if the overlapping image is darker than the background. If you put a dark letter over a light background, the knockout in the background would be choked, or reduced slightly so the dark letter would overlap the background

CMOS

Complementary metal-oxide semiconductors. A type of scanner sensor that is cheaper than a CCD, but less sensitive

CMYK

Four primary colors on a printing press: cyan, magenta, yellow, and black

Collect Fonts for Output

Gather all the different sets that were used in the document

Color Cast

When a scanner, camera, or printer makes an image appear to have an overall color hue. Old color photos from the 1960s often have an overall orange-yellow color cast

Color Correction

Where you change the image to ensure printable values, correct memory colors, and or for editorial reasons (changing the image to please the client)

Color Gamut

All the possible colors within a specific color space. If a color is in the RGB zone, but outside the CMYK zone, it is termed *out of gamut*

Color Management

Application of software to control the display and/or output of color on a variety of devices so that the result of all output matches the intended color representation

Color Management Module (CMM)

Engine used to drive any color conversion; functions like someone translating between languages. Profile is the dictionary and the CMM is the translator; results will vary depending on the CMM selected

ColorSync

Program that helps to set up the basic monitor space, which becomes the engine transitioning from RGB to CMYK

Commission International d'Eclairage (CIE)

Created a scientific color space in 1931, which was refined and named CIE L*a*b* in 1976. CIE attempted to define all color visible to an ideal human viewer in terms of three axes

Compression

Reduction in the size of a file by reducing the space required for storing the information in the file

Continuous Printing

On an inkjet printer, when the ink is sprayed constantly and is controlled by electronic deflectors

Continuous Tone

Images that contain a full range of grays (black-and-white photos) or color. Includes photographs, paintings, and almost anything you create in Adobe Photoshop

Contract Proof

Proof given to the client to sign as a form of a contract, implying that they agree with what they see on the proof and it is ready to go to press

Central Processing Unit (CPU)

Main computer chip used to manipulate and process data. Brain of the computer

Creep

Occurs when folded pages are inserted within each other; the more pages, the more space needed to fold around the center

Crop (Trim) Marks

Used to show the printer where you want the page to be trimmed. Trim marks need to be set to the final dimension of the page

Crossovers

Places where design elements cross the gutter of the page

Dandy Roll

Creates a watermark by shifting the paper fibers around to create a mark

Desktop Color Separation (DCS)

File format in which a single image is separated to create five files: a preview EPS file, and C, M, Y, and K separations

Debossing

Creative print finishing method in which the image is recessed into the page

Design Trapping

Adjustment of overlapping color objects to account for misregistration on a press

Desktop Proofs

Also called preliminary proofs, anything created to examine text, placement, or similar design issues. Not considered appropriate for contract proofing

Destination Profile

Profile of the printing device being used

Diecutting

Process that uses steel rules to cut shapes from paper and other materials to achieve visual or functional results

Digital Photography

Process of photographing an image onto disk instead of to a film negative

Digital Printing

Any printing that does not require a plate in order to image a substrate, including electrophotographic inking presses like the Indigo, desktop printers, and wide-format inkjet, to name a few

Digital Proofs

Proofs that are made directly from an electronic file

Distribute-and-Print

Model where the job is sent to printers around the country, printed locally, and mailed cheaply

Dithering

Mixing tiles of nearby colors

Dot Gain

Difference between a dark print and an acceptable print. Two kinds of dot gain, mechanical and optical. When the plate is exposed, light scatters a bit and can cause 3–5% *optical dot gain*. During the printing process, the paper and the printing process can cause the ink to spread, creating *mechanical dot gain* at a theoretical 50% dot

Downsampling

Similar technique to subsampling, but more scientific in its approach. Down-sampling looks at the array of pixels in your image and averages the values. The average is then assigned to the entire pixel area

DPI

Halftone dots per inch, usually referred to as dots per inch

Drop-On-Demand Printing
Occurs in inkjet printing; only sprays ink as it is needed

Dry Trapping
Term used to describe how overprinting inks adhere to each other when one ink is overprinted on an already-dry ink film

Electrophotography
Digitally controlled laser or a series of light-emitting diodes are used to create an invisible "image" of electrical charges on an imaging surface

Ellipses
Indicates to the reader that the person typing the text has deliberately omitted copy

Em Dash
Indicates a break in a sentence or a change in thought

Embedded Profile
Coded tag at the end of the image file data. It allows a color management module to translate the data correctly

Embossing
When an image is pressed into paper using heat and pressure. Paper is pressed between two dies, one raised (male) and the other recessed (female), which creates a raised image on the page. If the image is recessed in the page, it is called debossing

En Dash
Used in place of the word "through" or "to," as in a series of numbers

Encapsulated PostScript
PostScript file with a preview, used for storing vector and bitmapped artwork

End Papers
Sheets that connect the inside cover to the book block

Expert Set
Font that contains alternate type characters and numerals

Family
Group of typefaces under the same name in all sizes, postures, and weights

File Format
Structure of the data used to record line art and picture images

Flexography
Form of relief printing, uses a flexible plate typically made from photopolymer

Foil Stamping
Piece of colored foil placed between a piece of paper and a die. The die is heated and pressed against the foil and paper. Through the use of heat and pressure, the color layer from the foil is transferred onto the paper. The image remains flat

Foldability
Paper's ability to bend and fold

Font
Refers to any set of characters

Font Reserve
Font management program

Frequency Modulated (FM) Screening
Screening method in which halftone dots are created at a constant size; the number of dots in a specific area varies to create the illusion of dark and light tones. Commonly used with six-color (Hi-Fi) printing because moiré is not an issue.

Gamma
Lightness factor of image midtones

Gamut
Range

Gamut Map

When the colors that will print, or that will display on a monitor, are shown compared to the human visual spectrum

Gapless Cylinder

Gravure cylinder that allows the image to go completely around the cylinder, unlike lithography

Giclée Prints (pronounced 'jee-clay')

French for "sprayed ink" prints made with IRIS inkjet technology. Most of these inks are water-based and may fade over time. Some are pigment-based and better suited to archival

Glyph

Single character from a font

Grain Direction

Direction of the paper fibers in a sheet of paper. Called *grain long* if it runs along the longer dimension, and *grain short* if they run parallel to the shorter dimension

Graphical User Interface (GUI)

Way information is shown on screen; it is the interface used by the operating system to get things done, and includes icons or pictures, menus, and functions that allow easy system use

Gravure

Also called *rotogravure*, process of printing using a cylinder with holes in it

Grommeted

When a job has grommets, the edges are usually hemmed and metal eyelets are punched through the substrate. This allows for the insertion of strings to facilitate hanging the sign

Gutter

Inside margins of a bound product

Hairline Rules

Very thin lines that show in the design

Hard Proofs

Printouts made on a desktop printer. These are not used to evaluate color accurately

HDPI

Halftone dots per inch

Hi-Fi Printing

Printing option that includes extra colors, which increases the number of colors available for use. If your job requires exact colors, or neon or fluorescent colors, it may be worth the extra expense of a Hi-Fi print

Highlight

Brightest neutral white in an image that is not a reflection or a light source (light on water, or the sun itself)

Hue Error

Result of the inherent impurities of inks used in the printing process. Theoretically, 100% cyan and 100% magenta would create 100% blue. Hue error requires 100% cyan and 90% magenta to get a blue color

Hyphen

Used for minus signs, when a word is broken over two lines, or in compound words

Image Housing

Part of a digital press that contains carrier and toner particles. Carrier and toner are constantly churned inside the housing, which creates a negative (static) charge. The carrier particles remain in the housing as the brush stirs out toner particles, which are attracted to the positive (image) areas

Imagesetters

Laser printers that expose either film or light-sensitive printing plates

Imposition

Process of arranging the pages of your design in the proper order on the printing plates or imaging cylinder, so that when they are printed and folded, they will appear in the correct order

Ink Colors

Indicates the colorant set that will be used. SWOP is the default option

Ink Drawdowns

Ink smeared on the paper to show how the ink reacts on a specific paper

Input

Data you enter in your computer

International Color Consortium (ICC)

Group of companies that created color standardization practices for the graphic arts. All profiles of your scanner, printer, etc., are considered ICC profiles

Job Folder

Folder you create on your computer's desktop. Inside, it is helpful to create one folder for images, one for fonts, and leave the layout within the job folder but outside of the internal folders. This is one way to insure that your layout file links properly to images at all times

JPEG

Joint Photographic Experts Group, formed to create a standard for image compression. Also a type of file format

Kerning

Adjusting the space between letters

Knockout

When you place an object of one color over an object of another color. In order for the color of the top object to print correctly, the top object must knock out the bottom object, leaving white space where the top object prints

Liquid-Crystal Display (LCD)

Flat monitors that use florescent light, which projects through liquid crystals and color filters

Leading

Space between lines of type, measured from baseline to baseline

Letterpress

Form of relief printing

Ligature

Two or more letters joined as a single glyph

Light Diode Arrays (LDA)

LDA affects the dot size by attracting more or less toner particles, depending on the image. This means digital printing allows for bit depth as you print, which is why it is considered printing with pixels. LDA has 600 possible points of light per inch

Lightness (Luminance or L*)

One end of the L* axis is white, the other black, with a range from 1–100

Line Art

Usually black-and-white; includes drawings, graphics, charts, etc

Line Length

Length of a line measured in picas to achieve maximum readability

Line Spacing

Called leading; space between lines of type

Linear Array

Using a single row of sensors to gather color samples

Lossless Compression

Retains all pixel data for images; integrity is retained. This type of compression is recommended for high-contrast images, line art, and text. Lossless compression techniques used for PDF files are ZIP, CCITT Group 3 and 4, and run-length encoding

Lossy Compression

Uses algorithms to compress the file by selectively removing portions of the image (those details that the human eye does not pick out very well). Some of the image detail is lost, and artifacts or noise may be picked up in some images. Lossy techniques available in Acrobat Distiller are JPEG, subsampling, downsampling, and bi-cubic downsampling

Lines Per Inch (LPI)

Traditionally defined as the frequency of the screen placed in front of a graphic arts camera to create halftone dots from camera-ready copy; number of halftone dots that can exist in a linear inch

Laser Spots Per Inch (LSPI)

Number of spots produced by a laser imagesetter in a linear inch

LZW Compression

Designed to be able to compress all kinds of data, including images of varying bit depth

Magnification

Percentage you will be enlarging from the original

Main-Charge Scoratron

Wire that lays out a negative charge

Makeready

Anything involved in preparing a press or machinery for printing or binding

Mechanical Binding

Comb, and spiral or coil binding. Often used for presentation booklets because they are quick and easy to make. All forms of spiral binding allow the document to lay flat when open

Misregistration

When objects look slightly out of place; white spaces show up on the page

Mock-up

Rough version of a print job that is folded and numbered in order to check how to design with color in mind

Moiré

Interference pattern that happens when dots form a visible pattern within an image. Sometimes this happens when the picture has objects in a repeating pattern that end up interacting with the dots that make the image, creating a distracting pattern

Monitor Calibration Devices

Measures different color points and then adjusts them to target settings. The process is automatic and takes around 10 minutes. The advantage is that this is an objective calibration. Either stuck onto your monitor, or hang in front of it

Motherboard

Circuit board that peripherals and other computer components are plugged in to. Data is transmitted and received through the motherboard

Mottling

Visible non-uniformity in density, gloss, or color of printed ink

Multiple Masters

Base fonts that contain a master version of a typeface. A multiple master lets you alter the weight and dimensions of the face

Newsprint

Low-quality paper grade containing a lot of acidifying agents, which is why newsprint yellows over time. Other distinguishing characteristic is that newsprint soaks up ink like a sponge

Nip

Place where the gravure cylinder and the impression cylinder meet and pull the substrate through

Nip Pressure

Pressure created between the gravure and the impression cylinders

Non-Image Area

Part of the cylinder that does not have engraved cells and does not transfer ink to the substrate

On-Demand Printing

Printing a product as it is needed

Open Prepress Interface (OPI)

Extension to PostScript that automatically replaces low-resolution images with high-resolution images

OpenType

Compromise between PostScript and TrueType. It takes the strengths of each and adds even more features. The basic structure is that of TrueType, which means that OpenType has just one suitcase to package with your design job

Operating System (OS)

Maintains the flow of information from disk to computer and back again, to disk and then monitor, from keyboard or other input device to disk, to printer or other output device from disk, and so on. Basic tools such as booting, launching applications, file naming, copying, and access to peripherals such as monitors, drives, and scanners are controlled by the operating system

Orphan

Short sentence or word that is the last sentence or word of a paragraph, which is also the first line on the next page

Output Resolution

Line screen that will be used in creating the printing plates

Overprinting

Process of overlapping images without knocking out the color beneath

Packets

Envelope containing direct marketing materials

Paper Grade

Also referred to as a paper stock

Paper Spoilage Allowance

Amount of paper that is wasted in order to get the press up to color

Pasteboard

Area outside the document

Perceptual

Rendering intent that tells the computer to keep the range of colors in a photograph so that all the colors still look natural even if the numeric values switch

Phosphor

Substance in a cathode-ray tube that emits light when exposed to an electron beam

Photopolymer

Light-sensitive plastics

Photomultiplier Tube (PMT)

Electronic device, used in drum scanners, that produces electronic signals when exposed to light. The signals are converted to digital information that describes color value. Very sensitive to light variation, which results in the ability to capture small changes in tone

Point

Unit or measure in the graphic arts industry; 1 inch = 72 points

Portable Document Format (PDF)

Defined by Adobe as a file format that represents a document independent of the software, fonts, hardware, and operating system used to create it

PostScript

Page-description or computer programming language created by Adobe. PostScript, the most commonly used page-description language, was designed to improve text and graphic capabilities, and to control output devices, including printers and imagesetters

PostScript (Type 1) Fonts

Fonts that print smoothly on PostScript print devices. These have two or more elements to put in the font folder you provide the print bureau. A PostScript suitcase contains screen fonts that include hinting, which allows your fonts to be revealed on screen. There are also separate files not in a suitcase and which consist of an icon with a piece of the name of the font, a clue to help you know that they need to go along for the ride to the print provider

Pixels Per Inch (PPI)
Number of pixels along the side of one square inch in a computer

Pre-Charge Scoratron
Wire that lays out a negative charge of −650 volts

Preflighting
Process of checking electronic files to make sure that the necessary elements, including fonts and images, are present, and that all the necessary steps have been taken to make sure the file was created correctly

Press Proofs
First printed sheets off a press; often part of the press check, shows how the final product will look

Primary Colors
Basic color building blocks; in different color spaces, the building blocks are different, yet in the end they all interrelate

Print On-Demand
Jobs printed when you need them

Printer Spreads
Pages that face each other on an imposed press sheet; the arrangement of printer spreads, after the press sheet is folded, bound, and trimmed, creates reader spreads

Printing Plate
Surface, whether metal or a type of polymer, that is etched or chemically engraved to produce the image that is to be reproduced by a printing process

Process Color
Using four transparent ink colors to create full-color images. Four inks are cyan, magenta, yellow, and black, thus the name CMYK printing

Profile Editor Program
Software application that takes ideal, known values, and compares them with the values the calibrated device produces, measures the differences, and produces a profile

Profiling
Measures what a calibrated device is producing, calculates the difference between that and the ideal values, and produces a descriptive file to compensate for the differences. This file allows your system to compensate in order to produce the ideal values

Proof
Printed test sheet examined to check for flaws and errors. It also acts as a prediction of the results you will get off the press

Raised Wire Watermark
Image is raised on the dandy roll, which pushes paper fibers away to make the area look lighter

Raster Image Processor (RIP)
Hardware or software that converts your files into printable dots

Reader Spread
Pages that appear next to each other in the order they are to be in the final document

Reflective Scanner
Only scans photos, or non-transparent items. Light has to be reflected onto the CCDs in the scanner

Registration
Making sure that all the colors line up correctly and without any shifting

Registration Marks
Marks that help the printer ensure that the four color plates are lining up correctly during printing.

Re-imaged
Every time the drum in a digital printer rotates, even if the exact same image will be printed, it will be created again

Relative Colorimetric

Rendering intent used for graphics like logos. The computer factors in the white of the page, and tries to keep the numeric values of the color identical. This works well if all source colors are inside the gamut of the destination. If any colors are outside, they get clipped

Relief Printing

Uses raised image areas for printing, and uses pressure to imprint the image or text onto a substrate

Rendering Intents

Settings found in both ColorSync and Photoshop; lets you control how the computer performs a color conversion

RGB Space

Red, green, blue; the space in computer monitors, televisions, videos, and movies. Light starts white (like sunlight), then filters (like prisms) break it up into the primary colors of RGB

Right Reading

Image in the direction we normally read

River

Apparent white space that is the result of poor or random word spacing

Roughs

Sketches done at the second stage of a brainstorming session. After creating a number of thumbnails, this is the stage to generate larger sketches

Runability

Paper's ability to be printed without causing problems throughout the printing process

Saddle-Stitching

Method of binding in which the paper is folded, and the fold is stapled

Saturation

Usually used for business graphics to make each color as intense as possible

Scanning Resolution

Amount of samples per inch you need for the final version

Scoring

Strong impression on the paper to make folding easier

Secondary Colors

Result when you mix two primaries in equal proportions

Self-mailers

Simple one-page designs that are folded over once or twice, then mailed

Shadow

Darkest point in the image

Shadow Watermark

Image is impressed into the dandy roll and masks the area, which holds in more paper fibers to create a darker effect

Show-Through

Occurs when ink printed on one side of the paper or substrate can be seen through the paper on the other side

Signature

Large piece of paper that is folded, bound and trimmed to make the pages of a book

SNAP

Specifications for Newsprint Advertising Production

Soft Proofing

Method of proofing a document on a computer monitor instead of on a printed page

Solid Ink Density

Thickness of a layer of ink as read by a densitometer

Source Profile

Profile from the device that created a file. If you get the image from a Photo CD, the CD manufacturer should have a source profile. If you create the image on screen, your monitor profile would be the source

Specialty Printing

Printing of materials such as vinyl, wallpaper, floor coverings, and textiles

Spectrophotometer/ Densitometer

Hardware devices that measure how thick the layer of ink is, and what the color appears to be

Specular Highlights

Area of an image that is a natural light source or the reflection of a light source. Should not be considered when choosing the white point of an image

SPI

Samples per inch taken by the scanner

Spine Preparation

Book spine is filed down to expose the paper fibers so that they can be glued

Spot Color

Referred to as a custom, Pantone, or solid color, and is created on press with one ink rather than by combining cyan, magenta, yellow, and black inks

Spread

Process of enlarging one object slightly; used if the overlapping image, such as a letter, is lighter than the background. The lighter colored letter will be spread out and overlap the background slightly

Stationery Set

Letterhead, envelopes, and business cards

Steel Rule Diecutting

Used for larger dies and projects that need cuts closer in registration

Subsampling

Technique that evaluates the array of pixel data in your image and assigns a value for the entire area. The value of the centermost pixel of the area in your image is given to the surrounding pixels. The rest of the data is thrown away

Subtractive color

Printed colors achieved through cyan, magenta, yellow, and black (CMYK) inks, dyes, or toners. With ink on paper you start with the white (or base color) of the page; the more colors you pile on, the darker the color appears, so the color is subtracted during the viewing process

Suitcase

Font management program

SWOP

Stands for Specifications for Web Offset Publications. A set of standards developed by the magazine publishing industry and, for lack of other standards, became a frequent default option in the printing industry. It specifies for a particular grade of paper, a particular kind of press, and a certain set of inks

Tape Binding

Fabric tape with solid glue on one side is applied to the edge of the copies, wrapped around, and heated to melt the glue onto the edges of the paper

Tagged Image File Format (TIFF)

Most commonly used method for storing bitmap images in various resolutions, gray levels, and colors

Thumbnails

Small sketches of your initial design concepts. Should be only two inches tall

Tone Compression

Process of squeezing a larger gamut into a printable range

Total Ink Limit

In process printing, there are four colors, so the theoretical maximum total ink is 400%. For most press conditions, that number will oversaturate the paper and make it wet and wavy. SWOP default is 300%

Transfer Erase Duplex (TED)

Consists of four charged wires. The TEDs bounce the toner particles from negative to positive charges and back again as they move from one drum to the next. Charges are alternated between positive and negative to allow the toner to remain on the substrate

Transmissive Scan

Light goes through film as it scans. If a scanner can scan film or slides, it is a transmissive scanner

Trapping

Involves adjusting two adjacent colors that are different in order to avoid registration problems

TrueType

Type of font, based on quadratic curves, in which different sizes and weights of the font are contained in a single suitcase. Co-created by Apple and Microsoft, TrueType font are commonly used on the Windows platform

Type 3 Fonts

Adobe's public version that was missing some of the secret ingredients that make PostScript Type 1 fonts so well-crafted

Typeface

Overall design or look of a font. Typefaces are often named for their original designer, even if the specific version is a modern rendition. Bodoni and Jensen are examples

Tyvek

Material made from paper/plastic mix that yields a nearly unrippable substrate. Excellent for durable, lightweight banners

Under Color Addition (UCA)

Method which adds black in the place of cyan, magenta, and yellow that were removed by gray component replacement

Under Color Removal (UCR)

Method used by printers to retain image quality while using less ink. They find neutral values of cyan, magenta, and yellow inks and replace them with corresponding black values

Upsampling

Adding pixels to an existing image, with the intent of falsely increasing resolution

Variable Data

Information from a database that is fed into a layout template, used to create personalized or specialized versions of the layout

Variable-Data Printing

Printing process in which different information (data) is fed into a layout template, producing a single version of the template for each record in the data string

Viscosity

Ink's resistance to flow

Waterless Lithography

Uses a silicone plastic in non-image areas; the plastic repels the ink. It is the better option for printing with FM screens since it minimizes dot gain

Wet Trapping

Describes how overprinting inks adhere to each other when printed wet on wet. Each consecutive ink must adhere to the previous to produce the proper color

Widow

First line of a paragraph as the last line of a page or column

Workflow

Specific order in which a job is completed

Working Spaces

Whatever type of color mode you are currently in on a computer

Wrong Reading

Images or text that are reversed to how we normally read

INDEX

ABOUT THE AUTHORS

JESSICA BERLIN
received both a BFA in Photographic Illustration and an MS in Graphic Arts Publishing from the Rochester Institute of Technology. She has worked in the Creative Design Department at Fossil and is currently a prepress manager at Hasbro Inc. Jessica continues to work in graphic design and photography as a freelance artist.

CHRISTINA KIM
worked as a graphic designer for three years before getting her MS in Graphic Arts Publishing from the Rochester Institute of Technology. While working as in-house designer for Flower City Printing, she continues her work as a freelance designer, photographer, illustrator, and web designer. She received a Fine Arts degree from Hampshire College.

JENNIFER TALCOTT
received her BA in Communication Studies from the State University of New York College at Cortland and an MS from the Rochester Institute of Technology, where she studied Graphic Arts Publishing.

FRANK J. ROMANO
is a professor at the School of Print Media, Rochester Institute of Technology. He envisioned this publication and worked with the team of authors to develop it into an aid for graphic designers and print buyers.

ABOUT NAPL

NAPL is dedicated to helping the graphic arts community succeed within today's highly competitive communications environment. We help our members by offering educational, consulting, and member services, for both companies and individuals.

LEARN MORE ABOUT NAPL

www.napl.org

(Order online) Bookstore
http://store.napl.org

Membership Information
www.napl.org/napl/what_is_napl.htm

Contact Us
Phone: 800-642-6275
Fax: 201-634-0328
Email: Products@napl.org

75 West Century Road
Paramus, NJ 07652

ALSO AVAILABLE FROM NAPL

ALSO AVAILABLE FROM NAPL

ALSO AVAILABLE FROM NAPL